Organization Development

A Process of Learning and Changing

Second Edition

Organization Development

A Process of Learning and Changing

Second Edition

W. Warner Burke
Teachers College, Columbia University
W. Warner Burke Associates, Inc.

ADDISON-WESLEY PUBLISHING COMPANY
Reading, Massachusetts • Menlo Park, California • New York
Don Mills, Ontario • Wokingham, England • Amsterdam • Bonn
Sydney • Singapore • Tokyo • Madrid • San Juan • Milan • Paris

Library of Congress Cataloging-in-Publication Data

Burke, W. Warner (Wyatt Warner), 1935–
    Organization development : a process of learning and changing /
W. Warner Burke.
        p.   cm.   -- (The Addison-Wesley series on organization
development)
    Includes bibliographical references.
    ISBN 0-201-50835-4
    1. Organizational change.   I. Title.   II. Series.
HD58.8.B879   1993
658.4'06--dc20   93-14813
                                                          CIP

This book is in the Addison-Wesley Series on Organization Development.
Editors: Edgar H. Schein, Richard Beckhard

ISBN 0-201-50835-4
1 2 3 4 5 6 7 8 9 10-BA-9796959493

To Bobbi, Donovan, Courtney, and Brian

Other Titles in the Organization Development Series

Competing with Flexible Lateral Organizations, Second Edition

Jay R. Galbraith

1994 (50836)

This book focuses on creating competitive advantage by building a lateral capability, enabling a firm to respond flexibly in an uncertain world. The book addresses international coordination and cross business coordination as well as the usual cross functional efforts. It is unique in covering both cross functional (lateral or horizontal) coordination, as well as international and corporate issues.

The Dynamics of Organizational Levels: A Change Framework for Managers and Consultants

Nicholas S. Rashford and David Coghlan

1994 (54323)

This book introduces the idea that, for successful change to occur, organizational interventions have to be coordinated across the major levels of issues that all organizations face. Individual level, team level, inter-unit level, and organizational level issues are identified and analyzed, and the kinds of intervention appropriate to each level are spelled out.

Total Quality: A User's Guide for Implementation

Dan Ciampa

1992 (54992)

This is a book that directly addresses the challenge of how to make Total Quality work in a practical, no-nonsense way. The companies that will dominate markets in the future will be those that deliver high quality, competitively priced products and service just when the customer wants them and in a way that exceeds the customer's expectations. The vehicle by which these companies move to that stage is Total Quality.

Parallel Learning Structures: Increasing Innovation in Bureaucracies

Gervase R. Bushe and A.B. Shani

1991 (52427)

Parallel learning structures are technostructural interventions that promote system-wide change in bureaucracies while retaining the advantages of bureaucratic design. This text serves as a resource of models and theories built around five cases of parallel learning structures that can help those who create and maintain them be more effective and successful. For those new to parallel learning structures, the text provides practical advice as to when and how to use them.

Managing in the New Team Environment: Skills, Tools, and Methods

Larry Hirschhorn

1991 (52503)

This text is designed to help manage the tensions and complexities that arise for managers seeking to guide employees in a team environment. Based on an interactive video course developed at IBM, the text takes managers step by step through the process of building a team and authorizing it to act while they learn to step back and delegate. Specific issues addressed are how to give a team structure, how to facilitate its basic processes, and how to acknowledge differences in relationships among team members and between the manager and individual team members.

Leading Business Teams: How Teams Can Use Technology and Group Process Tools to Enhance Performance

Robert Johansen, David Sibbett, Suzyn Benson, Alexia Martin, Robert Mittman, and Paul Saffo

1991 (52829)

What technology or tools should organization development people or team leaders have at their command, now and in the future? This text explores the intersection of technology and business teams, a new and largely uncharted area that goes by several labels, including "groupware," a term that encompasses both electronic and nonelectronic tools for teams. This is the first book of its kind from the field describing what works for business teams and what does not.

The Conflict-Positive Organization: Stimulate Diversity and Create Unity

Dean Tjosvold

1991 (51485)

This book describes how managers and employees can use conflict to find common ground, solve problems, and strengthen morale and relationships. By showing how well-managed conflict invigorates and empowers teams and organizations, the text demonstrates how conflict is vital for a company's continuous improvement and increased competitive advantage.

Change by Design
Robert R. Blake, Jane Srygley Mouton, and Anne Adams McCanse
1989 (50748)

This book develops a systematic approach to organization development and provides readers with rich illustrations of coherent planned change. The book involves testing, examining, revising, and strengthening conceptual foundations in order to create sharper corporate focus and increased predictability of successful organization development.

Organization Development in Health Care
R. Wayne Boss
1989 (18364)

This is the first book to discuss the intricacies of the health care industry. The book explains the impact of OD in creating healthy and viable organizations in the health care sector. Through unique and innovative techniques, hospitals are able to reduce nursing turnover, thereby resolving the nursing shortage problem. The text also addresses how OD can improve such bottom-line variables as cash flow and net profits.

Self-Designing Organizations: Learning How to Create High Performance
Susan Albers Mohrman and Thomas G. Cummings
1989 (14603)

This book looks beyond traditional approaches to organizational transition, offering a strategy for developing organizations that enables them to learn not only how to adjust to the dynamic environment in which they exist, but also how to achieve a higher level of performance. This strategy assumes that change is a learning process: the goal is continually refined as organizational members learn how to function more effectively and respond to dynamic conditions in their environment.

Power and Organization Development: Mobilizing Power to Implement Change
Larry E. Greiner and Virginia E. Schein
1988 (12185)

This book forges an important collaborative approach between two opposing and often contradictory approaches to management: OD practitioners who espouse a "more humane" workplace without understanding the political realities of getting things done, and practicing managers who feel comfortable with power but overlook the role of human potential in contributing to positive results.

Designing Organizations for High Performance
David P. Hanna

1988 (12693)

This book is the first to give insight into the actual processes you can use to translate organizational concepts into bottom-line improvements. Hanna's "how-to" approach shows not only the successful methods of intervention, but also the plans behind them and the corresponding results.

Process Consultation, Volume 1: Its Role in Organization Development, Second Edition
Edgar H. Schein

1988 (06736)

How can a situation be influenced in the workplace without the direct use of power or formal authority? This book presents the core theoretical foundations and basic prescriptions for effective management.

Organizational Transitions: Managing Complex Change, Second Edition
Richard Beckhard and Reuben T. Harris

1987 (10887)

This book discusses the choices involved in developing a management system appropriate to the "transition state." It also discusses commitment to change, organizational culture, and increasing and maintaining productivity, creativity, and innovation.

Organization Development: A Normative View
W. Warner Burke

1987 (10697)

This book concisely describes and defines the theories and practices of organization development and also looks at organization development as change in an organization's culture. It is a useful guide to the field of organization development and is invaluable to managers, executives, practitioners, and anyone desiring an excellent overview of this multi-faceted field.

Team Building: Issues and Alternatives, Second Edition
William G. Dyer

1987 (18037)

Through the use of the techniques and procedures described in this book, managers and consultants can effectively prepare, apply, and follow up on the human processes affecting the productive functioning of teams.

The Technology Connection: Strategy and Change in the Information Age
Marc S. Gerstein

1987 (12188)

This is a book that guides managers and consultants through crucial decisions about the use of technology for increasing effectiveness and competitive advantage. It provides a useful way to think about the relationship between information technology, business strategy, and the process of change in organizations.

Stream Analysis: A Powerful Way to Diagnose and Manage Organizational Change
Jerry I. Porras

1987 (05693)

Drawing on a conceptual framework that helps the reader to better understand organizations, this book shows how to diagnose failings in organizational functioning and how to plan a comprehensive set of actions needed to change the organization into a more effective system.

Process Consultation, Volume II: Lessons for Managers and Consultants
Edgar H. Schein

1987 (06744)

This book shows the viability of the process consultation model for working with human systems. Like Schein's first volume on process consultation, the second volume focuses on the moment-to-moment behavior of the manager or consultant rather than on the design of the OD program.

Managing Conflict: Interpersonal Dialogue and Third-Party Roles, Second Edition
Richard E. Walton

1987 (08859)

This book shows how to implement a dialogue approach to conflict management. It presents a framework for diagnosing recurring conflicts and suggests several basic options for controlling or resolving them.

Pay and Organization Development
Edward E. Lawler

1981 (03990)

This book examines the important role that reward systems play in organization development efforts. By combining examples and specific recommendations with conceptual material, it organizes the various topics and puts them into a total systems perspective. Specific pay approaches such as gainsharing, skill-based pay, and flexible benefits are discussed and their impact on productivity and the quality of work life is analyzed.

Work Redesign
J. Richard Hackman and Greg R. Oldham

1980 (02779)

This book is a comprehensive, clearly written study of work design as a strategy for personal and organizational change. Linking theory and practical technologies, it develops traditional and alternative approaches to work design that can benefit both individuals and organizations.

Organizational Dynamics: Diagnosis and Intervention
John P. Kotter

1978 (03890)

This book offers managers and OD specialists a powerful method of diagnosing organizational problems and of deciding when, where, and how to use (or not use) the diverse and growing number of organizational improvement tools that are available today. Comprehensive and fully integrated, the book includes many different concepts, research findings, and competing philosophies and provides specific examples of how to use the information to improve organizational functioning.

Career Dynamics: Matching Individual and Organizational Needs
Edgar H. Schein

1978 (06834)

This book studies the complexities of career development from both an individual and an organizational perspective. Changing needs throughout the adult life cycle, interaction of work and family, and integration of individual and organizational goals through human resource planning and development are all thoroughly explored.

Matrix
Stanley M. Davis and Paul Lawrence

1977 (01115)

This book defines and describes the matrix organization, a significant departure from the traditional "one man-one boss" management system. The author notes that the tension between the need for independence (fostering innovation) and order (fostering efficiency) drives organizations to consider a matrix system. Among the issues addressed are reasons for using a matrix, methods for establishing one, the impact of the system on individuals, its hazards, and what types of organizations can use a matrix system.

Feedback and Organization Development: Using Data-Based Methods
David A. Nadler

1977 (05006)

This book addresses the use of data as a tool for organizational change. It attempts to bring together some of what is known from experience and research and to translate that knowledge into useful insights for those who are thinking about using data-based methods in organizations. The broad approach of the text is to treat a whole range of questions and issues considering the various uses of data as an organizational change tool.

Designing Complex Organizations
Jay Galbraith

1973 (02559)

This book attempts to present an analytical framework of the design of organizations, particularly of types of organizations that apply lateral decision processes or matrix forms. These forms have become pervasive in all types of organizations, yet there is little systematic public knowledge about them. This book helps fill this gap.

Organization Development: Strategies and Models
Richard Beckhard

1969 (00448)

This book is written for managers, specialists, and students of management who are concerned with the planning of organization development programs to resolve the dilemmas brought about by a rapidly changing environment. Practiced teams of interdependent people must spend real time improving their methods of working, decision making, and communicating, and a planned, managed change is the first step toward effecting and maintaining these improvements.

Organization Development: Its Nature, Origins, and Prospects
Warren G. Bennis

1969 (00523)

This primer on OD is written with an eye toward the people in organizations who are interested in learning more about this educational strategy as well as for those practitioners and students of OD who may want a basic statement both to learn from and to argue with. The author treats the subject with a minimum of academic jargon and a maximum of concrete examples drawn from his own and others' experience.

Developing Organizations: Diagnosis and Action
Paul R. Lawrence and Jay W. Lorsch
1969 (04204)

This book is a personal statement of the authors' evolving experience, through research and consulting, in the work of developing organizations. The text presents the authors' overview of organization development, then proceeds to examine issues at each of three critical interfaces: the organization-environment interface, the group-group interface, and the individual-organization interface, including brief examples of work on each. The text concludes by pulling the themes together in a set of conclusions about organizational development issues as they present themselves to practicing managers.

About the Author

W. Warner Burke is Professor of Psychology and Education at Teachers College, Columbia University, and Chairman of W. Warner Burke Associates, Inc., a consulting firm specializing, in part, in OD. He was formerly the editor of *Organizational Dynamics,* associate and book editor of *Journal of Applied Behavioral Science,* and editor of *Academy of Management Executive.* He has a B.A. from Furman University and an M.A. and Ph.D. from the University of Texas, Austin. Dr. Burke is a Fellow of the Academy of Management, a member of the American Psychological Society, the Society of Industrial and Organizational Development, and has been on the Board of Governors of both the Academy of Management and the American Society for Training Development. He is a diplomate in industrial/organizational psychology, American Board of Professional Psychology.

Foreword

The Addison-Wesley Series on Organization Development originated in the late 1960s when a number of us recognized that the rapidly growing field of "OD" was not well understood or well defined. We also recognized that there was no one OD philosophy, and hence one could not at that time write a textbook on the theory and practice of OD, but one could make clear what various practitioners were doing under that label. So the original six books launched what has since become a continuing enterprise, the essence of which was to allow different authors to speak for themselves instead of trying to summarize under one umbrella what was obviously a rapidly growing and highly diverse field.

By the early 1980s the series included nineteen titles. OD was growing by leaps and bounds, and it was expanding into all kinds of organizational areas and technologies of intervention. By this time, many textbooks existed as well that tried to capture core concepts of the field, but we felt that diversity and innovation were still the more salient aspects of OD.

Now as we move into the 1990s our series includes over thirty titles, and we are beginning to see some real convergence in the underlying assumptions of OD. As we observe how different professionals working in different kinds of organizations and occupational communities make their case, we see we are still far from having a single "theory" of organization development. Yet, a set of common assumptions is surfacing. We are beginning to see patterns in what works and what does not work, and we are becoming more articulate about these patterns. We are also seeing the field increasingly connected to other organizational sciences and disciplines such as information technology, coordination theory, and organization theory. In the early 1990s we saw several important themes described with Ciampa's *Total Quality* showing the important link to employee involvement in continuous improvement, Johansen et al.'s *Leading Business Teams* exploring the important arena of electronic information tools for teamwork, Tjosvold's *The Conflict-Positive Organization* showing how conflict management can turn conflict into constructive action, Hirschhorn's *Managing in the New Team Environment* building bridges to group psychodynamic theory, and Bushe and Shani's *Parallel Learning Structures* providing an integrative theory for large-scale organization change.

We continue this trend with two revisions and one wholly new approach. Burke has taken his highly successful *Organization Development* into new realms with an updating and expansion. Galbraith has updated and enlarged his classic theory of how information management is at the heart of organization design with his new edition entitled *Competing with Flexible Lateral Organizations,* and Rashford and Coghlan have introduced the important concept of levels of organizational complexity as a basis for intervention theory in their book entitled *The Dynamics of Organizational Levels.*

We welcome these revisions and new titles and will continue to explore the various frontiers of organization development with additional titles as we identify themes that are relevant to the ever more difficult problem of helping organizations to remain effective in an increasingly turbulent environment.

New York, New York Richard H. Beckhard
Cambridge, Massachusetts Edgar H. Schein

Preface

My purpose with this book is to provide an overview of the field of organization development (OD). I have written the book with at least three audiences in mind: (1) the manager, executive, or administrator—a potential user of organization development; (2) the practitioner in the field of OD—a user who may need some guidelines for his or her practice either as a consultant internal to an organization or as an external consultant working with a variety of clients; and (3) the student—one who may in the future use the information provided in either of roles (1) or (2).

While no sea change has occurred in the field of OD since my earlier books were published in 1982 and 1987, enough has changed that this later version was in order. All chapters have been revised and two new ones added.

Some of the eleven chapters will be more pertinent to the OD practitioner than to the manager. The following synopsis of each chapter will signal some of these differences in emphasis and should help the reader make choices, should time and interest be limited. First though, a word of qualification and clarification.

Although I believe I have been objective in describing OD, the theories underlying the field, and the way OD practitioners typically work, I do represent a bias. I do have a position about what I think OD *should* be: I define OD in part as change of an organization's culture. Not everyone in the field agrees with me. Whether you the reader believe one way or the other (or whether you even care!) should not prevent a reasonable understanding of how I have described the concepts and practice of organization development.

Chapter 1, What Is Organization Development?, presents an actual case, a previous consulting assignment of mine that I believe succinctly illustrates the primary characteristics of OD practice (although it does not exemplify what OD really is—or should be—taking into consideration my bias).

Chapter 2, Organization Development Then and Now, provides context for the field by considering OD today, comparing it with the past, and then relating OD to future trends in the organization of tomorrow.

Chapter 3, Where Did OD Come From?, traces the roots or forerunners of the field as well as briefly describes ten theories related to organizational behavior that underlie OD practice.

Chapter 4, Organization Development as a Process of Change, covers the fundamental models of change that guide OD practitioners and, using another actual case to illustrate, also covers the phases of consultation that OD practitioners follow in their practice.

Chapter 5, Defining the Client: A Different Perspective, addresses the question of who the client is, which may seem obvious but isn't. This perspective considers the client in terms of relationships.

Chapter 6, Understanding Organizations: The Process of Diagnosis, describes some of the most common frameworks or organizational models that OD practitioners use after they have conducted their interviews and perhaps administered questionnaires, made their observations, and read some documents and then attempted to make systematic sense out of what often at first seems a mass of confusing data.

Chapter 7, The Burke–Litwin Model of Organizational Performance and Change, extends and builds on the previous chapter by describing my own way of thinking about organizations and changing them. The significant change that occurred at British Airways during the latter half of the 1980s is explained to illustrate how the Burke–Litwin model was used as a framework.

Chapter 8, Planning and Managing Change, explains what OD practitioners do after the diagnostic phase and includes many of the primary steps involved in managing change as well as theory about organizational culture change.

Chapter 9, Does OD Work?, presents some summary evidence that it does, highlights the issues in evaluating OD efforts, and provides the key reasons for conducting an evaluation.

Chapter 10, The OD Consultant, covers consultant roles and functions, abilities required of an OD practitioner, OD values, and ways to become an OD practitioner.

Chapter 11, New Dimensions of Organization Development, the final chapter, is both a current assessment and a look to the future of OD. Once again, OD values are considered and, finally, some conclusions are made about the future of the field.

Having previously written a textbook on OD (Burke, 1982), I have drawn from it to write this book, especially the parts describing the practice of organization development, including a couple of case examples and explanations of the theories that have contributed to the field.

Richard Beckhard and Edgar Schein, two of the most experienced and respected persons in OD, were reviewers of the manuscript that eventually became this book. It would be difficult, if not impossible, to find reviewers who could equal their critique and insight. My sincere appreciation is gratefully offered.

My assistant, Mary Zippo, was invaluable in translating my handwriting to typed page. She has mastered the word processor. I doubt if I ever will, so thank God for Mary!

Pelham, New York   W. W. B.

Contents

1

What Is Organization Development?

The term *organization development,* or OD, the label most commonly used for the field, has been in use since at least 1960. In the '60s and early '70s, jokes about what OD abbreviated meant were common. Today few people in the world of large organizations associate OD with overdose, olive drab, or officer of the day, however. Organization development as a field may not yet be sufficiently known to be defined in the dictionary or explained in the *Encyclopedia Britannica,* but it has survived some turbulent times and will be around for the foreseeable future. Explaining what OD is and what people do who practice OD continues to be difficult because the field is still being shaped to some degree and because the practice of OD is more of a process than a step-by-step procedure. That is, OD is a consideration in general of how work is done, what the people who carry out the work believe and feel about their efficiency and effectiveness, rather than a specific, concrete, step-by-step linear procedure for accomplishing something.

An example should help to explain. The following case represents a fairly strict, purist stance for determining what OD is and what it is not.

A Case

The client organization was a division of a large U.S. manufacturing corporation. The division consisted of two plants, both of which manufactured heavy electrical equipment. The division was in trouble at the time I was hired as OD consultant. There were quality and control problems and customers were complaining. The complaints concerned not only poor quality but late delivery of products—inevitably weeks, if not months, later than promised. Several weeks prior to my arrival at the divisional offices, a senior vice-president from the corporation's headquarters had visited with the division's top management team, a group of six men. The corporate VP was very much aware of the problems, and he was anything but pleased about the state of affairs. At the end of his visit he made a pronouncement, stating in essence that, unless this division were "turned around" within six months, he would close it down. This ultimatum would mean loss of jobs for more than 1000 people, including, of course, the division's top management team. Although the two plants in this division were unionized, the corporate VP had the power and the support from his superiors to close the division if he deemed it necessary.

For several months before this crisis the division general manager had taken a variety of steps to try to correct the problems. He had held problem-solving meetings with his top management team; he had fired the head of manufacturing and brought in a more experienced man; he spent time on the shop floor talking with first-line supervisors and workers; he authorized experiments to be conducted by the production engineers to discover better methods; and he even conducted a mass rally of all employees at which he exhorted them to do better. After the rally, signs were placed throughout the division announcing the goal: to become number 1 among all the corporation's divisions. None of these steps seemed to make any difference.

The general manager also sought help from the corporate staff of employee relations and training specialists. One of these specialists made several visits to the division and eventually decided that an outside consultant with expertise in organization development could probably help. I was contacted by this corporate staff person, and an exploratory visit was arranged.

My initial visit, only a few weeks after the corporate vice-president had made his visit and his pronouncement, consisted largely of (1) talking at length with the general manager, (2) observing briefly most of the production operations, (3) meeting informally with the top management team so that questions could be raised and issues explored, and, finally, (4) discussing the action steps I proposed. I suggested we start at the top. I would interview each member of the top management team at some length and report back to them as a group what I had diagnosed from these interviews; then we would jointly determine the appropriate next steps. They agreed to my proposal.

A couple of weeks later, I began by interviewing the six members of the top management team (see Fig. 1.1) for about an hour each. They gave many reasons for the division's problems, some of the presumed causes contradicting others. What became apparent was that, although the division's goals were generally understandable, they were not specific enough for people to be clear about priorities. Moreover, there were interpersonal problems, such as conflict between the head of marketing and the head of employee relations. (The marketing manager believed that the employee relations manager was never forceful enough, and the employee relations manager perceived the marketing manager as a blowhard.) We decided to have a two-and-a-half-day meeting of the top management team at a hotel some ninety miles away to work on clarifying priorities and ironing out some of the interpersonal problems.

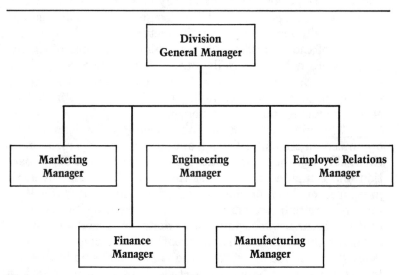

Figure 1.1
Organization Chart: Top Management Team of Manufacturing Division

The off-site meeting was considered successful because much of what we set out to accomplish was achieved—a clearer understanding of the problems and concerns and an agenda for action. The crucial problem did indeed surface. A layer or two of the organizational onion had been peeled away, and we were finally getting at not only some causes but specifics that we could address with confidence that we were moving in the right direction. The key problem that surfaced was the lack of cooperation between the two major divisional functions—engineering and manufacturing.

As the organization chart in Fig. 1.1 shows, the division was organized according to function. The primary advantages of a functional organization are clarity about organizational responsibilities because of the division of labor and the opportunities for continuing development of functional expertise within a single unit. The disadvantages also stem from the distinct divisions of responsibility. Since marketing does marketing and manufacturing manufactures, the twain rarely meet. In this case, the problem was between engineering and manufacturing. The design engineers claimed that the manufacturing people did not follow their specifications closely enough, while the manufacturing people claimed that the design engineers did not consider that the machinery for manufacturing was old and worn. Because of the condition of the machinery, the manufacturing people were not able to follow the design engineers' specifications to the desired tolerances. Each group blamed the other for the drop in overall product quality and for the delays in delivery of the product to the firm's customers.

This kind of conflict is common in organizations that are organized functionally. The advantages of such organization are clear, of course, but a premium is placed on the need for cooperation and communication across functional lines. Moreover, the pressures of daily production schedules make it difficult for managers to pull away and clearly diagnose the situation when conflicts occur between functions. Managers spend a great deal of time fighting fires—that is, treating symptoms rather than causes. An outside consultant who is not caught up in this day-to-day routine can be more objective. Thus my primary role as consultant to this division was diagnostician.

The next step was to deal with this problem of intergroup conflict. Another off-site meeting was held about a month later with the top six people from engineering and their equivalent number from manufacturing. These men were predominantly engineers, either design engineers assigned to the engineering function or production engineers working in the manufacturing operation. These two functions were supposed to interact closely. The design engineers sent blueprint-like plans to manufacturing for production of the specified electrical equipment. The manufacturing people reiterated their complaint that the design tolerances were too stringent for their worn-out machinery to handle. Meeting the design specifications would require purchasing new machinery, but the cost was prohibitive. "And besides," they added, "those design guys never set foot on the shop floor anyway, so how would they know whether we complied with their specs or not?"

These comments and the attitudes they reflect are illustrative and common. Communication is rarely what it should be between groups in such organizations. It is also common, perhaps natural, for functional groups to distance themselves from one another to protect their own turf.

Using a standard OD intergroup problem-solving format, I worked with the two groups to understand and clarify their differences, to reorganize the two groups temporarily into three four-person cross-functional groups to solve problems, and to plan specific action steps they could take to correct their intergroup problems. The object in such a format is to provide a procedure for bringing conflict to the surface to enable those affected to understand it and manage a solution more productively. An initial exchange of perceptions allows the parties to see how each group sees itself and the other group. Next comes identification of the problems that exist between the two groups. Finally, mixed groups of members from both functions work together to plan action steps that will alleviate the conflict and solve many of the problems. See "Managing Conflict Between Groups" (Burke, 1974) for a detailed description of this process and see Fig. 1.2 for a summary of its application in this case.

The outcome of this intergroup meeting clearly suggested yet another step. A major problem needing immediate attention was that the manufacturing group was not working well as a team. The design engineers produced evidence that they often got different answers to the same design production problem from different manufacturing people. Thus, the next consulting

Procedure to Resolve Conflict

Participants

Manufacturing Department (six people)	Engineering Design Department (six people)

Step 1: Identify Perceptions

Each department's six representatives work as a group and separately from other departments to generate three lists: how we see ourselves, how we see them, and how we think they see us.

Step 2: Exchange of Perceptions

Meeting as total community of twelve, each departmental group of six presents its lists of perceptions to the other departmental group.

Step 3: Problem Identification

Employing information presented in Step 2, the two groups, again working separately, identify the primary problems that exist between the two departments.

Step 4: Problem Exchange

Each group presents its problem list to the other group.

Step 5: Problem Consolidation

The total group, or representatives from each department, consolidate the two lists into one.

Step 6: Priority Setting

Together the twelve people rank the problems listed from most to least important.

Step 7: Group Problem Solving

The total community is reorganized into three cross-departmental, temporary problem-solving groups. Each of the three groups, consisting of four people, two from manufacturing and two from engineering design, takes one of the top three most important problems and generates solutions.

Step 8: Summary Presentations

Each of the three groups presents its solutions to the other two groups.

Step 9: Follow-up Planning

Final activity in total community of twelve is to plan implementation steps for problem solutions.

Figure 1.2
Example of Intergroup Problem-Solving Process

step was to help conduct a team-building session for the top group of the manufacturing function. Approximately two months after the intergroup session, I met off-site for two days with the production engineers and general foremen of manufacturing. In this session, we set specific manufacturing targets, established production priorities, clarified roles and responsibilities, and even settled a few interpersonal conflicts.

By this time I had been working with the division on and off for close to nine months. After my team-building session with the manufacturing group, I was convinced that I had begun to see some of the real causes of the divisional problems; until then I had been dealing primarily with symptoms, not causes. I noticed, for example, that the first-line supervisors had no tangible way of rewarding their hourly workers; they could use verbal strokes—"Nice job, Alice," or "Keep up the good work, Joe"—but that was about it. They could use negative reinforcement, however, if they so chose—for example, threatening a one- or two-week layoff without pay if performance did not meet standards. This type of action was within the bounds of the union contract.

The hourly employees were paid according to what is called a measured day-work system. Their pay was based on what an industrial engineer had specified as an average rate of productivity for a given job during an eight-hour day. Incentive to produce more for extra pay was not part of the system.

I suggested to the division general manager that a change in the reward system might be in order. At that suggestion, the blood seemed to drain from his face. He explained that the present president of the corporation was the person who, years before, had invented the measured day-work system. He did not believe in incentive systems. The division general manager made it clear that he was not about to suggest to the corporate president, the big boss, that the measured day-work system should perhaps be scrapped. I discussed this matter with my original corporate contact, the staff specialist. He confirmed the origin of the reward system and stated that changing the reward system was not an option. I became extremely frustrated at this point. I thought that I had finally discovered a basic cause of divisional, if not corporate, production problems, but it became apparent that this root of the problem was not going to be dug up. The next step I nonetheless recommended in the overall problem-solving process—to change some elements of the reward system for hourly employees, if not the entire system— was not a step the division general manager was willing to take. The corporate staff person was also unwilling to push for change in this aspect of the system. My consulting work with the division ended shortly thereafter.

The point of this consultation case is as follows: What I used as a consultant was the standard methodology of organization development, but the project was *not,* in the final analysis, organization development. Having described the case, I will now use it as a vehicle for clarifying what OD is and what it is not.

Definitions

In the consultation, I used OD methodology and approached the situation from an OD perspective. The methodological model for OD is *action research;* data on the nature of certain problems are systematically collected and then action is taken as a function of what the analyzed data indicate. The specific techniques used within this methodological model (few of which are unique to OD) were:

1. *Diagnosis.* Interview both individuals and groups, observe the situation, then analyze and organize the data collected.
2. *Feedback.* Report back to those from whom the data were obtained on the organization's collective sense of the organizational problems.
3. *Discussion.* Analyze what the data mean and then plan the steps to be taken as a consequence.
4. *Action.* Take those steps.

In OD language, taking a step is making an *intervention* into the routine way in which the organization operates. In the consultation case there were three primary interventions: team building with the division general manager and the five functional heads who reported directly to him, intergroup conflict resolution between the engineering and manufacturing groups, and team building with the top team of the manufacturing group.

The case does not qualify as an effort in OD because it meets only two of the three criteria for OD as I have defined them (Burke and Hornstein, 1972, p. xviii). For change in an organization to be OD it must (1) respond to an actual and perceived need for change on the part of the client, (2) involve the client in the planning and implementation of the change, and (3) lead to change in the organization's culture.

As a consultant I was able to meet the first two criteria but not the third. For cultural change to have taken place in this case, the reward system would have to have been modified. The bias presented in this book is that *organization development is a process of fundamental change in an organization's culture.* By fundamental change, as opposed to fixing a problem or improving a procedure, I mean that some significant aspect of an organization's culture will never be the same. In the case described, it was the reward system. In another case, it might be a change in the organization's management style, requiring new forms of exercising authority, which in turn would lead to different conformity patterns, since new norms would be established, especially in decision making.

Now that we have jumped from a specific case to more general concepts, perhaps we should slow down and define some terms. Any organization, like any society, has its own unique culture. A given culture consists of many elements, but the primary element is the unique pattern of norms, standards, or rules of conduct to which members conform. Other significant elements of an organization's culture are its authority structure and way of exercising power, values, rewards and way of dispensing them, and communication patterns.

My definition of culture emphasizes norms and values because doing so gives us an operational understanding of culture: conforming patterns of behavior. Norms can be changed. The changed behavior is a different conformity. This position, albeit perhaps limited, is nevertheless consistent with Kurt Lewin's thinking concerning change in a social system (Lewin, 1958; see Chapter 3 of this book).

Edgar Schein (1985) defines culture at a "deeper" (emphasis added) level, as

> *basic assumptions* and *beliefs* that are shared by members of an organization, that operate unconsciously, and that define in a basic "taken-for-granted" fashion an organization's view of itself and its environment. These assumptions and beliefs are learned responses to a group's

problems of *internal integration*. They come to be taken for granted because they solve those problems repeatedly and reliably. This deeper level of assumptions is to be distinguished from the "artifacts" and "values" that are manifestations or surface levels of the culture but not the essence of the culture. (pp. 6–7)

According to Schein's definition, I am dealing with surface levels. And this is true—almost. The OD practitioner's job is to elicit from the client implicit norms, those conforming patterns that are ubiquitous but are just below the surface, not salient. These behaviors are *manifestations* of basic assumptions and beliefs as Schein notes, and may not be the essence but constitute more operational means for dealing with organizational change.

At the outset of an organization consultation it is practically impossible for an OD practitioner to deal with data other than fairly superficial behavior. To discover the essence of organizational culture, the practitioner must establish not only good rapport with members of the client organization but also a sound basis for trust. If organization members are reluctant or even unwilling to talk openly, the OD practitioner may never discover the true culture. To find out why its members behave the way they do, the OD practitioner must therefore truly engage the client organization's members. This is done by asking discerning and helpful questions and by showing genuine interest in the members as people and in what they do, what they are responsible for, what their problems are, and what helps or hinders them from making the kind of contribution they want to make as well as what will be beneficial to the organization. Engaging people in this way is an *intervention* into the organization, not simply observation.

Schein (1991) terms this form of organizational consultation and research "clinical research." He maintains that one cannot understand the culture of an organization via the traditional scientific model, that is, making observations and gathering data without disturbing the situation. It is practically impossible to collect data without disturbing the situation. The classic Hawthorne studies, as Schein appropriately points out, demonstrated rather clearly that changes observed were due more to the researcher's presence than to any of the other modifications in the workers' environment, for example, change in lighting.

Schein's point, therefore, is this: To discover the essence of culture the practitioner must *interact* with the client—ask questions, test hypotheses, and provide helpful suggestions. He states that "once the helping relationship exists, the possibilities for learning what really goes on in organizations are enormous if we learn to take advantage of them and if we learn to be good and reliable observers of what is going on" (p. 5).

In summary, the OD practitioner begins with asking about and observing norms and values in the client organization. Inherent in this process is building rapport and trust with the client organization as well as testing the values and norms presented and observed. Gradually, then, the OD practitioner becomes clearer about the essence of the culture and can sort out what needs to be maintained, if not strengthened, and what needs to change.

For an organization to develop, then, change must occur, but this does not mean that *any* change will do. Using the term *development* to mean change does not, for example, mean growth. Russell Ackoff's distinction is quite useful and relevant to our understanding of what the "D" in OD means:

> Growth can take place with or without development (and vice versa). For example, a cemetery can grow without developing; so can a rubbish heap. A nation, corporation, or an individual can develop without growing.... [Development] is an increase in capacity and potential, not an increase in attainment.... It has less to do with how much one has than with how much one can do with whatever one has. (Ackoff, 1981: 34–35)

OD, therefore, is a process of bringing to the surface those implicit behavioral patterns that are helping and hindering development. Bringing these patterns of conformity to organization members' conscious awareness puts them in a position to reinforce the behaviors that help development and change those that hinder. OD practitioners help clients to help themselves.

More specifically, OD practitioners are concerned with change that integrates individual needs with organizational goals more fully; change that improves an organization's effectiveness through better utilization of resources, especially human resources; and change that involves organization members more in the decisions that directly affect them and their working conditions.

At least by implication and occasionally directly, I shall define OD several times throughout this book. The following general definition provides a starting point: Organization development is a planned process of change in an organization's culture through the utilization of behavioral science technologies, research, and theory.

What if an organization's culture does not need any change? Then OD is neither relevant nor appropriate. Organization development is not all things to all organizations. It is useful only when some fundamental change is needed. Then how does one recognize when fundamental change is needed? Perhaps the clearest sign is when the same kinds of problems keep occurring. No sooner does one problem get solved than another just like it surfaces. Another sign is when a variety of techniques is used to increase productivity, for example, and none seems to work. Yet another is when morale among employees is low and the cause can be attributed to no single factor. These are but a few signs. The point is that OD ultimately is a process of getting at organizational root causes, not just treating symptoms.

To be clear: Much of what is called OD is the use of OD techniques—off-site team building, training, facilitation of ad hoc meetings, providing private and individual feedback to managers and executives, and so on—but not in my purist definition. According to my definition organization development provides fundamental change in the way things are done, modifying the essence of organizational culture. Many, perhaps most, practitioners, therefore, are conducting sessions and processes that rely on OD technology—and that's fine. But using OD techniques is not necessarily providing organization development.

A Total System Approach

The target for change is the organization—the total system, not necessarily individual members (Burke and Schmidt, 1971). Individual change is typically a consequence of system change. When a norm, a dimension of the organization's culture, is changed, individual behavior is modified by the new conforming pattern. Organization development is a total system approach to change.

Most practitioners agree that OD is an approach to a total system and that an organization is a sociotechnical system (Trist, 1960). Every organization has a technology, whether it is producing something tangible or rendering a service; a subsystem of the total organization, technology represents an integral part of the culture. Every organization is also composed of people who interact to accomplish tasks; the human dimension constitutes the social subsystem. The emphasis of this book is on the social subsystem, but both subsystems and their interaction must be considered in any effort toward organizational change.

The case at the beginning of this chapter illustrates the sociotechnical qualities or dimensions of an organization. The problem between the engineering and manufacturing groups was both technical (out-of-date machinery) and social (lack of cooperation). The case also illustrates another important point. A cardinal rule of OD is to begin any consultation with what the client considers to be the problem or deems critical, not necessarily what the consultant considers important. Later the consultant can recommend or advocate specific changes, but the consultant begins as facilitator.

Whether the consultant's role should encompass advocacy as well as facilitation is in dispute within the field of OD. Practitioners and academicians are divided according to their views of OD as contingent or as normative. The contingent camp argues that OD practitioners should only facilitate change; according to their view the client determines the direction of change, and the OD practitioner helps the client get there. The normative camp, significantly smaller, argues that, although the approach to OD should be facilitative at the beginning, before long the practitioner should begin to recommend, if not argue for, specific directions for change. I place myself in the normative camp, the minority. Although I am taking a position, I shall make every attempt to be comprehensive and as objective as possible in my coverage of OD.

In the consultative case introduced previously, I dealt almost exclusively for more than nine months with what the client considered to be the central problems and issues. As I became more confident about what I considered to be not just symptoms but causes, I began to argue for broader and more directed change. Until then we had been putting out fires, not stopping arson. Although the organization was correcting problems, it was not learning a different *way* of solving problems— that is, learning how to change, the essence of OD. This essence has been elaborated on by Argyris and Schön (1978), who call it "organizational learning," and more recently by Senge (1990). According to Senge, for organizational learning to occur, members and especially managers and executives must develop systems thinking. To understand complex managerial problems one has to visualize the organization as a whole, how one aspect of the system affects another within an overall pattern. These ideas are highly compatible and consistent with what I mean by OD.

When a consultant takes a position, regardless of how well founded, he or she risks encountering resistance. This obviously happened in the case I described earlier. I didn't consult much longer than the first nine months. As it turned out, I did help; the division did turn around in time to keep the corporate vice-president from acting on his threat to close the plant unless quality and delivery time were improved. As a consultant, I take satisfaction in this outcome. From an OD perspective, however, I consider that my work was a failure. That assessment stems from two perspectives, one concerning research and the other concerning values.

Research evidence regarding organizational change is now very clear. Change rarely if ever can be effected by treating symptoms, and organizational change will not occur if effort is directed at trying to change individual members. The direction of change should be toward the personality of the organization, not the personality of the individual. My knowledge of the research evidence, my realization in the consultation case that a modification in the organization's reward system was not likely, and my acceptance that OD, by definition, means change led me to conclude that, in the final analysis, I had not accomplished organization development.

The values that underlie organization development include humanistic and collaborative approaches to changing organizational life. Although not all OD practitioners would agree, decentralizing power is part of OD for most organizations. In the consultation case, it seemed that providing first-line supervisors with more alternatives for rewarding their workers positively not only was more humanistic but would allow them more discretionary and appropriate power and authority for accomplishing their supervisory responsibilities. Changing the reward system was the appropriate avenue as far as I was concerned, but this change was not to be and, for my part, neither was OD.

What I have just stated is likely to raise many more questions than answers. Let us move on now to more clarity and, I hope, answers. In the next chapter, we shall explore a broader context for OD as a way of clarifying further the work of OD practitioners and the domain of their work for the future.

2

Organization Development Then and Now

The original Addison-Wesley OD series, published in 1969, consisted of six volumes. These books represented one of the first attempts to define the field of organization development, the field at the time being at most a decade old. Much has changed since then. Let us consider what has happened since 1969 that has had the most impact on the field of OD and what the future trends in organizations are likely to be.

Some Significant Changes Since 1969

Perhaps the most significant event to affect the field of OD, at least from an economic if not competence perspective, was the oil embargo and recession of 1972–73. Organizations cut back, especially in the "soft" areas of training and human resource development. Many OD consultants had to change labels. The less experienced and less competent were weeded out. Today OD practitioners, especially those who survived the economically tough times around 1973 and remained in OD, are more competent. Those newer to the field have taken advantage of the greater pool of knowledge about OD to learn quickly the concepts and skills required to practice OD effectively. Today's group of OD practitioners is larger than two decades ago, and whether veterans or newcomers, seems to be more competent.

With respect to organizational dynamics and approaches to management in general, there have been at least nine significant shifts since 1969 (Table 2.1).

From Growth to Decline to Consolidation

Perhaps the biggest change is that organizational growth, while not a thing of the past, is far more limited today. Growth is limited to certain industries and entrepreneurial activities and is not nearly as widespread as during the 1960s. Moreover, competition today is far keener than a quarter of a century ago and occurs not just from around the corner, but worldwide. The current pressure on many businesses is to become *global;* they must not only be more efficient but be able to compete more effectively.

In addition to the global movement, I find that *consolidation* is a primary goal of corporate management today. It is as if a decade later executives are vigorously following the advice of Peters and Waterman (1982) to stick to one's knitting. Executives today are working harder to determine their corporations' core business and then to shed those divisions that do not fit the defined core. It also seems that core or not, many businesses are being shed simply because of their inadequate profitability.

Table 2.1
Significant Shifts in Organizational Dynamics and Management Since 1969

From	To
Growth	Consolidation
Moderate speed	Warp speed
Moderate complexity	High complexity
Strategic planning	Strategic implementation
Consultant jargon	Popular, accepted concepts
Management	Leadership
Unilateral, top-down management	Multilateral, participative management
Little concern for ethics	High concern for ethics
Micro	Macro

Another form of consolidation is the merger or acquisition. This form of consolidation is occurring in the pharmaceutical industry, which has traditionally involved a great many firms with a strong market leader. Merck & Co., for example, accounts for less than 20 percent of the world market; the remainder of the market is divided among hundreds of other players. In such an industry, some "joining up" is only logical (Burke and Jackson, 1991).

The movement from managing growth toward managing consolidation has implications for the organization consultant. In 1969 we did a lot of team building; today even more is required. Consultants must be highly knowledgeable and skilled about such matters as:

- The psychological consequences of "downsizing"—layoffs—on both employees who are let go and those who remain. (See, for example, Brockner, 1988; and Brockner et al., 1986.)

- Downsizing with the least amount of psychological pain (Brockner, 1992).

- Designing and managing flatter organizational structures. The old maxim that an optimum span of control is 7, 8, or 9 is just that—*old*. OD consultants today must know how to help managers deal with 15, 20, or even 50 direct reports, not a mere 7 subordinates. This means, for example, that they must be knowledgeable about semiautonomous and self-managed work groups (Hackman, 1989).

- Defining core competencies required to execute a corporation's core businesses. This requires on the part of OD consultants (1) knowledge about the business and (2) the ability to determine (by means of interview, observational, and analytical skills) whether individual organizational members possess the requisite competencies.

- The particular nature of the client's business itself, the larger industry in which the business is a player, and the primary factors that cause ups and downs in that industry, such as seasonal differences, changing government regulations, and changing technology. A CEO recently told me that the number 1 value of his human resource chief (a Ph.D. I/O psychologist) was the fact that he knows, studies, and cares about the business.

This list provides only a taste of the knowledge and skills OD consultants need to work effectively in today's leaner, flatter, tighter, and bottom-line focused organizations.

Time: From Moderate to Warp Speed

Everything seems to be at a faster pace these days, even organization change. Change occurs rapidly when precipitated by traumatic events such as a leveraged buyout, an acquisition, a sudden downturn in the market, or a scandal. Even organizational cultures seem to change more rapidly today. Although not everyone is convinced that culture can be changed at all, I am convinced. Having been involved from 1985 to 1990 in the effort of British Airways (BA) to change from a government agency to a private corporation, it is clear to me that significant change in BA's culture did indeed occur (Goodstein and Burke, 1991) in just five years.

In a related effort that shaped a newly merged culture from two different businesses (in somewhat the same industry) and two different nationalities (British and American), the time required was less than three years (see Burke and Jackson, 1991).

Unequivocal documentation of the comparative times needed for culture change is not possible and is less to the point than the fact that applying what we have learned about culture change (see, for example, the recent book by Kotter and Heskett, 1992) may expedite change. It is clear that executive clients expect faster change. Moreover, CEOs themselves these days rarely have five or more years to manage such a change.

Those of us who claim to be organization consultants must be knowledgeable about the nature of organization culture (see such books as Deal and Kennedy, 1982; Sashkin and Kiser, 1993; Schein, 1985; Frost et al., 1991) and skillful in applying such knowledge (see, for example, Lawler, 1992; Nadler et al., 1992).

Unlike the way many of us were trained, we cannot wait for more evidence before offering advice or direction to clients. Although the client may seem to be moving too rapidly, without sufficient documentation, even half-cocked, we as consultants are expected to respond, to help. Managers today are admonished to be innovative, to take risks, and to act more quickly. We must take risks as well.

From Moderate Complexity to Even Greater Complexity

Twenty-five years ago organization change was complex enough, but I naively thought that someday I would master the complexity. However, it seems that no matter how much complexity I comprehend, organizations continue to become even more complex, so I remain behind. The best way I can describe these newer, more recent complexities is in the form of paradoxes. Let me begin by quoting Rosabeth Kanter (1989: 20–21). She expressed what I mean quite eloquently when she identified incompatible, paradoxical demands that are placed on today's managers and executives, demands such as:

- Be entrepreneurial and take risks—but don't cost the business anything by failure.
- Continue to do everything you're currently doing, even better—and spend more time communicating with employees, serving on teams, and launching new products.
- Speak up, be a leader, set the direction—but be participative, listen well, cooperate.
- Succeed, succeed, succeed—and raise terrific children.

Corporations as well face escalating and seemingly incompatible demands, according to Kanter:

- Get "lean and mean" through restructuring—while being a great company to work for and offering employee-centered policies, such as job security.
- Encourage creativity and innovation to take you in new directions—and "stick to your knitting."
- Communicate a sense of urgency and push for faster execution, faster results—but take more time to deliberately plan for the future.

I add to the list of paradoxes, several slanted more toward the OD consultant's world:

- We organizational and psychological consultants are becoming specialists even as organizational conceptualization is moving more toward systemic and holistic thinking.

- Organization members experience more stress than ever due to change and, consequently, have a desire for some stability, yet chaos is more likely to be the new norm.
- With tougher times facing most organizations, *how* one manages is as important as achieving results.
- Organizational members cry out for leadership and direction yet demand more participation.
- There is more talk than ever about vision, mission, new directions, values, and promises to customers, yet one of the most significant issues concerning top management today is that so many managers and executives do *not* "walk the talk," as the expression goes.
- Competition in business is keener than ever, yet there is a clear movement afoot, especially in mature industries, to join with the enemy via strategic alliances and joint ventures—witness IBM and Apple.
- OD consultants seem to be moving more toward "traditional management consulting" (that is, concern with business matters) and traditional consultants seem to be moving more toward the "soft" domains (that is, concern with process issues).

One way to respond to the paradoxes is to educate yourself in areas that are foreign to your domain of expertise in order to gain a broader perspective. Three such areas have been helpful to me:

Understanding Oneself. While training as a Gestalt therapist some years ago I learned the concept of polarities. Through therapeutic experiences, I became comfortable with an initially discomfiting notion and in due course read more. Being reasonably comfortable with either a polarity or a paradox is helpful in today's world of organization consulting.

Understanding the Universe. Prior to the popularity of chaos theory, I ran across an article in my favorite magazine at that time, *Saturday Review* (now defunct), by Fritjof Capra (1977). A physicist, he explained that protons and neutrons were not particles as we normally think of them, but waves of probability interconnection. Thus atomic physics does not concern "things" but a "complicated web of relations between the various parts of a unified whole" (Capra, 1977: 23). Capra based his article on an earlier, marvelous book, *The Tao of Physics* (Capra, 1976) and later expanded on that theory with another, *The Turning Point* (Capra, 1983). Organizational behavior, too, seemed to me to be more like waves and interconnections than entities or events (Burke, 1980). Later, when chaos theory became popularized, I dug in, studying Gleick (1987), for example. I have recently found another book by Wheatley (1992) that is much easier to read and oriented more toward organizational behavior.

Understanding Change. I have been struck by the theorizing of Ilya Prigogine and the subsequent writings of Erich Jantsch (1980). They state that to understand evolution, one must focus more on disequilibrium than on equilibrium, the implication being that change is not linear. Jantsch also contends that evolution is accelerating, just as the overall process of change appears to be. This theory has been heralded by some as a paradigmatic shift comparable to Einstein's move away from Newton.

Just as Einstein's theory of relativity wrested the physical sciences away from Newton's static ideas of gravity, Jantsch's ideas challenge us to view movement, relativity, and change in living systems as *constant*. He argues that all living things are always co-evolving, yet maintaining a "relativity" to one another. Both Jantsch and Prigogine believe that the disequilibrium and perturbation that arise from time to time in living things are actually a kind of "molting," a shedding of the old within organisms as they strive to attain a higher level of existence. These perturbations, activities of disequilibrium, are signs of positive change that lead to self-organization rather than to decline. (See Chapter 5 for more elaboration on the work of Capra, Prigogine, and Jantsch.)

From an organization change perspective, this theory reminds me of Greiner's (1972) ideas about the life cycle of organizations as well as the work of Adizes (1979). I am convinced that organization change should occur like a perturbation or a leap in the life cycle of the organization, not as an incremental process. The management of the change should be incremental, but not the initiation of the change itself.

Another way to gain perspective and not feel trapped by an organizational paradox or dilemma is deliberately and conscientiously to seek new and different consulting experiences and not remain doing solely what you do well. My typical consulting assignment is with a large corporation, or at least some part of a large corporation. Recently I took an assignment with a small (about 130 people), new (started in 1987) business in an industry about which I know very little.

The chairman and founder, a scientist, is at an impasse with the president, who is an experienced, professional manager recruited from the same industry. To some extent, the issues are classic—the clash between science and the commercialization of products—yet the personalities involved, with their particular values and viewpoints, biases, and idiosyncrasies, are unique.

Addressing conflict between people is not new to me; sorting out the basis of these conflicts in terms of which decisions are or should be science-driven as opposed to commercial-driven, and whether we are in a power struggle that is ideological rather than political, or vice versa, is not exactly old hat for me. But this conflict situation is rather recalcitrant. I hope I am learning. I think I am. Am I helping? We'll see; it is still too early to tell. It is, after all, quite complex.

From Strategic Planning to Strategic Implementation

Strategic planning is not passé, but executives have learned that planning is about 10 percent of the effort to change an organization, whereas implementing the plan, the tougher part of the job by far, requires the remaining 90 percent of the effort. Thus, managing change is the emphasis today (see Chapter 7).

From Consultant Jargon to Popular, Accepted Concepts

The language of organizations has changed. Twenty-five years ago my clients would ask what I meant by *culture;* today they use the term before I do. *Value* is another term that clients use before I do as well as *vision, mission, climate,* and *leadership.* I welcome this language change yet I am uneasy about it because even after thirty years of OD I am not certain that I truly understand these terms or concepts. Do clients really understand these terms they so loosely bandy about?

Clients today use OD jargon quite easily yet are very uneven in their level of understanding and commitment to the action the words betoken. Thus while they all may use the words, not all act on them. Even though most use the terms, some remain skeptical about if not resistant to change.

From Management to Leadership

In 1969, leadership was not mentioned very often. It was not considered unimportant, but the term simply was seldom used. Today, leadership and its distinctions from management are discussed and debated frequently (see, for example, Bennis and Nanus, 1985; Burke, 1986; Zaleznik, 1977). The leadership function is not only highlighted more today, it is emphasized in the context of bringing about organizational change (see Tichy and Devanna, 1986).

From Unilateral, Top-Down Management to Multilateral, Participative Management

Organizational members today are less tolerant of the arbitrary use of power than was true in the past. And while conflict resolution and effectiveness in lateral relations were acknowledged as important in 1969, they are viewed by most executives as critical for effective organizational functioning today. This shift is due in part to (1) more decentralized authority and flatter hierarchies, where getting work done depends more on influence skills than on the exercise of power as a function of status or position; (2) the emphasis being given to collaborative, joint approaches to labor-management relations as opposed to adversarial ones; and (3) the occurrence of mergers and acquisitions, where achieving integration or at least some degree of smooth working relationships is important.

From Little Concern for Ethics to a High Concern for Ethics

In part, at least, increased competition has no doubt caused some managers to cut corners. Scandals either occur more frequently today or they are more likely to be exposed than was true in the past. Many managers are therefore caught in the vise (if not paradox) between meeting targets more rapidly than ever before and with less cost and emphasizing high quality. The two do not have to be mutually exclusive. In fact, managers are perhaps more wary about short-term measures, knowing that in the long run a large price will be paid one way or the other. Yet, they feel the pressure.

OD consultants are on occasion put in the position of serving as conscience for the client. This is an uncomfortable role, to be sure, but can be quite helpful. Sometimes managers simply need to be reminded of the ethics of a situation. When reminded, they often feel relieved that someone will support their doing the right thing.

From a Micro Perspective to a Macro

The shift from micro to macro perspective since 1969 is perhaps more specific to the practice of OD than to management or organizational dynamics in general. In the 1960s OD practitioners viewed organizational issues mostly in terms of individuals and small groups (sensitivity training, T-groups, management development), whereas today OD practitioners take a larger, more systematic perspective (reward systems, strategic planning, structure, management information systems). This shift is far more realistic for purposes of organizational change.

The nine shifts described here are not the only ones since 1969, but they are the most significant for OD. OD practitioners are in the business of change and they involve people in decisions and activities that directly affect them. These nine shifts concern in various ways organization change and differences in the way people are managed.

One last shift concerns power and politics in organizations. OD practitioners today are more willing to accept these organizational dynamics as realities and more willing to attempt to take them into account when facilitating the management of change.

The New Corporation

To broaden our context regarding changes since 1969 let us consider the work of two current and highly popular writers on the organizational scene—John Naisbett and Tom Peters. Naisbett's best seller *Megatrends* (1982) caused readers to think about the changing nature of organizations. His later book, co-authored with Patricia Aburdene (Naisbett and Aburdene, 1985), was more to the point of organizational shifts, however. The following list is their observations of how today's corporation is being "re-invented":

1. The best and brightest people will gravitate toward those corporations that foster personal growth.

2. The manager's role is that of coach, teacher, and mentor.

3. The best people want ownership—psychic and literal—in a company; the best companies are providing it.

4. Companies will increasingly turn to third-party contractors, shifting from hired labor to contract labor.

5. Authoritarian management is yielding to networking, people-style management.

6. Entrepreneurship within the corporation—"intrapreneurship"—is creating new revitalizing companies inside out.

7. Quality will be paramount.

8. Intuition and creativity are challenging the "It's all in the numbers" business school philosophy.

9. Large corporations are emulating the positive and productive qualities of small business.

10. The dawn of the information economy has fostered a massive shift from infrastructure to quality of life (pp. 45–46).

Tom Peters, another astute observer of the organizational scene, also covers the significant shifts he sees in the ways corporations do their business today. He has discussed these shifts in terms of "old to new" across the primary organizational functions. Table 2.2 is a summary of his observations (Peters, 1987).

The third observer and researcher of organizations, Rosabeth Moss Kanter, has been especially interested in managing innovation. In *The Change Masters* (1984), she writes about

Table 2.2
Shifts of Organizational Culture Over Time

Old	New
Manufacturing	
Emphasis on volume; low cost and efficiency more important than quality and responsiveness; capital and automation more important than people	Emphasis on short production runs; people as important or more so than capital and automation; quality and responsiveness critical; manufacturers as business team members, not just functional specialists; joint problem solving with suppliers
Marketing	
Mass marketing, advertising, and data analysis; lengthy market tests; highly competitive to achieve market share; analysis more important than intuition; consideration of large projects only	Fragmented markets, new uses; market creation rather than market sharing; rapid data collection; marketers in the field; innovations via listening to customers; heightened awareness of service
Sales and Service	
Move the product; volume is king; product ideas from marketing and engineering, not sales; service as mechanics, not primary source of customer listening	Sales as relationship management higher priority than volume; sales and service prime input to new product and new service development
International	
Adjunct activity; way to move post-peak U.S. designated and manufac-	Primary activity; focus on new market creation not just lagging follow-up

(continued)

Table 2.2   *(continued)*

Old	New
tured products; "global brands" managed by U.S. headquarters marketers	use of U.S. product; extensive off-shore product development; more mandatory overseas assignments

Innovation

Central R&D as driver; big products the norm; technology science driven, not market/ customer driven; cleverness of design more important than reliability, maintainability, and serviceability	All activities represent potential for innovation —manufacturing, MIS, personnel, accounting—big ends from small beginnings; flatter, more responsive organizations; all functions to the field,with customers, multifunction teams as opportunity creators

People

Capital more important than people; scale economies the priority; no way to beat turnover problem, therefore training is a waste; unions a dragging force; money is the only motivator; employee share ownership only works when stock price is rising	Quality service and responsiveness through people more than through capital; participation programs; gainsharing programs; extensive training

Organization

Hierarchical, staff centered; officially matrixed to solve coordination needs; span of control 1:10 at the lowest levels	Flat, large span; 1 to 100; line dominated; business team, group-focused smaller facility sizes (250 instead of 1000 people); strategy making bottom-up, decentralized; no group executives

(continued)

Table 2.2 *(continued)*

Old	New
	MIS
Centralized information control; central MIS fiefdom as information hoarders for the sake of "consistency"	Decentralized data processing connected by local area networks with access to all other data banks; central MIS as staff advisers for the strategic use of information, e.g., direct customer/supplier/ company linkage
	Financial Management and Control
Centralized; staff as reviewer of all proposals; formulator of extensive guidance—staff as the police	Decentralized; almost all financial people in the field; finance members of business team and entrepreneurial skunk works; high spending authority at facility/ business unit level
	Leadership
Detached, analytic; centralized strategy planning dominated by central corporate and group executive staffs	Values set from top, strategic development from below; all staff functions decentralized; value driven; leader as dramatist/tone setter/visionary

her findings of innovative practices and patterns across a number of organizations. Pertinent to our consideration here, she lists eight characteristics of innovative organizations:

1. Work responsibilities described in terms of results, with flexibility in the way they are achieved

2. Unallocated resources, such as time or money, available for projects beyond formal job descriptions and business plans

3. Abundant and visible recognition for a variety of achievements, not just a few occasional rewards for superstars

4. Ongoing budgets for frequent and continuing education and training, plus special assignments that challenge and stretch people

5. An emphasis on communicating business plans, market conditions, and other information through all levels, with advance warning of possible policy shifts

6. Lots of cross-fertilization, with opportunities to transfer into a variety of departments or business units

7. A networking structure, through special project teams, to bring together people at various levels in different departments or business units

8. Frequent trials of new concepts and new ideas, with most people involved in and committed to at least one new initiative a year

---

Summary

All of these observers and researchers of organizations, Naisbett and Auberdene, Peters, and Kanter, believe that effective organizations have the following characteristics:

- They are less hierarchical in structure and they "network" more to get work done and to communicate.
- They involve organizational members in decisions they are expected to implement.
- They are, in general, more people oriented.

Both Peters and Kanter stress the importance of three qualities: (1) flexibility in how work is done, that is, allowing as much autonomy as possible, (2) everyone being an innovator, and (3) greater information flow. Naisbett and Auberdene also overlap with Kanter in highlighting the increased emphasis on providing development opportunities and activities for organizational members.

If we consider the points of overlap and agreement among these organizational observers and researchers as strong indicators of organizational effectiveness today and in the near future, and if I am reasonably accurate about the nine shifts that have occurred over more than two decades, then OD practitioners have a bright and exciting future.

People identified with the field of organization development have consistently advocated involving people in decisions that directly affect them. Trends now support this position. They have been identified with humanistic means of dealing with members of organizations. Trends now support these approaches and values too. Being process oriented, OD practitioners have been identified with more flexible ways of communicating and conducting work, have facilitated networking activities, and have been advocates of personal development and growth for organization members.

It should be clear after reading the next chapter that OD's history and theoretical roots are closely linked to much of what is being advocated by observers and researchers of organizational effectiveness today.

3

Where Did OD Come From?

Evolution is a better term than *birth* to characterize the beginnings of OD as a singular event. This chapter thus traces the evolution of OD from its forerunners and selected theoretical roots.

Before OD

Even in evolution we must start somewhere. There was no "big bang" or "blessed event" in OD, but considering three forerunners or precursors will help us to understand the beginnings, that is, where OD came from. These three precursors are sensitivity training, sociotechnical systems, and survey feedback.

Sensitivity Training

From an historical perspective, it would be interesting to know how many events, inventions, and innovations that occurred around 1946 had lasting impact through the subsequent decades. Apparently once World War II ended, people felt free to pursue creative endeavors. Both sensitivity training, later "housed" at the National Training Laboratories (NTL), and a similar yet different version of human relations training independently founded at the Tavistock Institute in London, began about that time.

On the U.S. side, sensitivity training, or the T-group ("T" for training, or laboratory training), all labels for the same process, consisted and still consists today of small group (eight to ten people) discussions in which the primary, almost exclusive source of information for learning is the behavior of the group members themselves. The feedback participants receive from one another regarding their behavior becomes a source of personal insight and development. Participants also learn about group behavior and intergroup relationships.

T-groups are educational vehicles for individual change. During the late 1950s, when this form of education began to be applied in industrial settings for organizational change, the T-group became one of the earliest so-called interventions of organization development.

Sensitivity training began to be used as an intervention for organizational change. Members of the small T-groups were either organizational "cousins"—from the same overall organization but not within the same vertical chain of the organization's hierarchy—or members of the same organizational team, so-called family groups. Douglas McGregor of the Sloan School of Management at the Massachusetts Institute of Technology (MIT) conducted this kind of training at Union Carbide. Similar events at Esso and at the Naval Ordnance Test Station at China Lake, California, represented the early forms of organization development, which usually took the form of what we now call team building (Burck, 1965; McGregor, 1967).

During the same period McGregor and Richard Beckhard were consulting with General Mills. Working on what we now call a sociotechnical systems change, they helped to change some of the work structures at the various plants to introduce more teamwork and decision making at the shop-floor level. Although they fostered more "bottom-up" management, they didn't want to call what they were doing "bottom-up." Nor were they satisfied with "organization development," the label that became the name for the work Herb Shepard, Harry Kolb, Robert R. Blake, and others were doing at the Humble Refineries of Esso. Nevertheless McGregor and Beckhard called what they were doing organization development. Meanwhile across the Atlantic at the Tavistock Institute, the label sociotechnical system stuck.

Sociotechnical Systems

In the United Kingdom at about the same time that sensitivity training began in the United States, Eric Trist and Ken Bamforth of the Tavistock Institute were consulting with a coal mining company. They found that coal was mined by teams of six. Each team selected its own members and performed all tasks from extraction of the coal to loading to getting it to the surface. Teams were paid on the basis of group effort and unit productivity, not individual effort, and tended to be quite cohesive.

Problems arose with the introduction of new equipment and a change in technology that changed the way work was conducted. Individual, not group, labor became the norm. As work became more individualized and specialized and jobs more fractionated, productivity decreased and absenteeism increased.

Trist and Bamforth suggested combining the essential social elements of the previous, team mode of work with the new technology. When the company's management implemented their suggestions, productivity rose and absenteeism decreased. The specifics of this early work, including the documented measurements and outcomes, are reported in Trist (1960) and Trist and Bamforth (1951). Similar work was done by A. K. Rice, another Tavistock consultant and researcher, in two textile mills in Ahmedabad, India (Rice, 1958).

The approach pioneered by the Tavistock consultants is based on the premise that an organization is simultaneously a social and a technical system. Whether they produce something tangible or render a service, all organizations have technology, a subsystem of the total organization and an integral part of the culture. All organizations also are composed of people who interact around a task or series of tasks, and this human dimension constitutes the social subsystem. The emphasis of OD is typically on the social subsystem, but it should be clear that both subsystems and their interaction must be considered in any effort toward organizational change.

Survey Feedback

Organization development has been influenced by industrial/organizational psychology. This influence is perhaps manifested most in the third precursor to OD, survey feedback. Rensis Likert, the first director of the Institute for Social Research of the University of Michigan, started by founding the Survey Research Center in 1946. Kurt Lewin had founded the Research Center for Group Dynamics at MIT. With his untimely death in 1947, the Center was moved to the University of Michigan later that year. These two centers initially constituted

Likert's institute. The two primary thrusts of these centers, questionnaire surveys for organizational diagnosis and group dynamics, combined to give birth to the survey feedback method. As early as 1947 questionnaires were being used systematically to assess employee morale and attitudes in organizations.

One of the first of these studies, initiated and guided by Likert and conducted by Floyd Mann, was done with the Detroit Edison Company. From their work on the problem of how best to use the survey data for organization improvement, the method we now know as survey feedback evolved. Mann was key to the development of this method. He noted that, when a manager was given the survey results, any resulting improvement depended on what the manager did with the information. If the manager discussed the survey results with his subordinates yet failed to plan certain changes for improvement jointly with them, nothing happened—except, perhaps, an increase in employee frustration with the ambiguity of having answered a questionnaire and never hearing anything further.

Briefly, the survey feedback method involves, first, the survey, collecting data by questionnaire to determine employees' perceptions of a variety of factors, most focusing on the management of the organization. The second step is the feedback, reporting the results of the survey systematically in summary form to all people who answered the questionnaire. Systematically, in this case, means that feedback occurs in phases, starting with the top team of the organization and flowing downward according to the formal hierarchy and within functional units or teams. Mann (1957) referred to this cascade as the "interlocking chain of conferences." The chief executive officer, the division general manager, or the bureau chief, depending on the organization or subunit surveyed, and his or her immediate group of subordinates receive and discuss feedback from the survey first. Next, the subordinates and their respective groups of immediate subordinates do the same, and so forth downward until all members of the organization who had been surveyed hear a summary of the survey and then participate in a discussion of the meaning of the data and the implications. Each functional unit of the organization receives general feedback concerning the overall organization and specific feedback regarding its particular group. Following a discussion of the meaning of the survey results for their particular group, the boss and his or her subordinates then jointly plan action steps for improvement. Usually, a consultant meets with each of the groups to help with data analysis, group discussion, and plans for improvement.

This is a rather orderly and systematic way of understanding an organization from the standpoint of employee perceptions. Processing this understanding back into the organization so that change can occur, with the help of an outside resource person, not only was a direct precursor to and root of organization development, it is an integral part of many current OD efforts.

Current OD efforts using survey feedback methodology do not, however, always follow a top-down, cascading process. The survey may begin in the middle of the managerial hierarchy and move in either or both directions, or may begin at the bottom and work upward, as Edgar Schein (1969) has suggested. For more information about and guidelines for conducting survey feedback activities, see David Nadler's book in the Addison-Wesley OD series (Nadler, 1977).

Finally it should be noted that there are other forerunners or precursors to OD. A case in point is the activity prior to World War II at the Hawthorne Works of Western Electric. There Mayo (1933), Roethlisberger and Dickson (1939), and Homans (1950) established that psychological and sociotechnical factors make significant differences in worker performance.

The work at Hawthorne and its consequent impact occurred some two decades prior to the three precursors I chose to discuss in some detail. Thus, sensitivity training, sociotechnical systems, and survey feedback had a much greater and more direct influence on the beginnings of OD.

Theoretical Roots

Organization development has other roots in the area of concepts, models, and theories. What follows is a synopsis of some of the thinking of a fairly select group of people who have helped to provide most of the theoretical and conceptual underpinnings of OD. Ten theorists or conceptualizers were selected to represent the theory associated with OD because no single theory or conceptual model is representative or by itself encompasses the conceptual field or the practice of OD. We have instead a group of minitheories that have influenced the thinking and consultative practice of OD practitioners; each helps to explain only a portion of organizational behavior and effectiveness.

Ten theory categories were selected because they best represent the theory we do have within the field of OD. Some prominent names in the field of OD were not included because their contributions have been more descriptive than theoretical (an example is Blake and Mouton's 1964 *Managerial Grid*). The selection is a matter of judgment and could be debated. In fact, I have heard Frederick Herzberg state that he did not associate himself with the field. B. F. Skinner probably never heard of organization development. In other words, these theorists did not elect themselves into OD. I have chosen them because I believe their thinking has had a large impact on the practice of OD.

Need Theory—Maslow and Herzberg

According to Maslow (1954), human motivation can be explained in terms of needs that people experience to varying degrees all the time. An unsatisfied need creates a state of tension, which releases energy in the human system and, at the same time, provides direction. This purposeful energy guides the individual toward some goal that will respond to the unsatisfied need. The process whereby an unsatisfied need provides energy and direction toward some goal is Maslow's definition of motivation. Thus, only unsatisfied needs are motivating; a satisfied need creates no tension and therefore no motivation.

Maslow contended that we progress through a five-level need system one level at a time. The hierarchy represents a continuum from basic or physiological needs to safety and security needs to belonging needs to ego-status needs to a need for self-actualization.

It is on this last point, a single continuum, that Herzberg parts company with Maslow. Herzberg (1966; Herzberg, Mausner, and Snyderman, 1959) maintains that there are two continua, one concerning dissatisfaction and the other concerning satisfaction. It may be that the two theorists are even more fundamentally different in that Herzberg's approach has more to do with job satisfaction than with human motivation. The implications and applications of the two are much more similar than they are divergent, however.

Herzberg argues that only the goal objects associated with Maslow's ego-status and self-actualization needs provide motivation or satisfaction on the job. Meeting the lower-order needs simply reduces dissatisfaction; it does not provide satisfaction. Herzberg calls the goal objects associated with these lower-level needs (belonging, safety, and basic) hygiene or maintenance factors. Providing fringe benefits, for example, prevents dissatisfaction and thus is hygienic, but this provision does not ensure job satisfaction. Only motivator factors, such as recognition, opportunity for achievement, and autonomy on the job ensure satisfaction.

Herzberg's two categories, motivator factors and maintenance or hygiene factors, do not overlap. They represent qualitatively different aspects of human motivation.

One other point of Herzberg's is important: He states that not only does the dimension of job dissatisfaction differ psychologically from job satisfaction, but it is also associated with an escalation phenomenon, or what some have called the principle of rising expectations: The more people receive, the more they want. This principle applies only to job dissatisfaction. Herzberg uses the example of a person who receives a salary increase of $1000 one year and then receives only a $500 increase the following year. Psychologically, the second increase is a cut in pay. Herzberg maintains that this escalation principle is a fact of life, and that we must live with it. Management must continue to provide, upgrade, and increase maintenance factors—good working conditions, adequate salaries, and competitive fringe benefits—but should not operate under the false assumption that these factors will lead to greater job satisfaction.

Job enrichment, a significant intervention within OD and a critical element of quality-of-work-life projects, is a direct application of Herzberg's theory and at least an indirect one of Maslow's.

Expectancy Theory—Lawler and Vroom

Expectancy theory (Lawler, 1973; Vroom, 1964) has yet to have the impact on organization development that need theory has had, but it is gaining in acceptance and popularity. This approach to understanding human motivation focuses more on outward behavior than on internal needs. The theory is based on three assumptions:

1. People believe that their behavior is associated with certain outcomes. Theorists call this belief the *performance-outcome expectancy*. People may expect that, if they accomplish certain tasks, they will receive certain rewards.

2. Outcomes or rewards have different values (*valence*) for different people. Some people, for example, are more attracted to money as a reward than others are.

3. People associate their behavior with certain probabilities of success, called the *effort-performance expectancy*. People on an assembly line, for example, may have high expectancies that, if they try, they can produce 100 units per hour, but their expectancies may be very low that they can produce 150 units, regardless of how hard they may try.

Thus, people will be highly motivated when they believe that their behavior will lead to certain rewards, that these rewards are worthwhile and valuable, and that they are able to perform at a level that will result in the attainment of the rewards.

Research has shown that high-performing employees believe that their behavior, or performance, leads to rewards that they desire. Thus, there is evidence for the validity of the theory. Moreover, the theory and the research outcomes associated with it have implications for how reward systems and work might be designed and structured.

Job Satisfaction—Hackman and Oldham

Hackman and Oldham's (1980) *work design model* is grounded in both need theory and expectancy theory. Their model is more restrictive in that it focuses on the relationship between job or work design and worker satisfaction. Although their model frequently leads to what is called job enrichment, as does the application of Herzberg's motivator-hygiene theory, the Hackman and Oldham model has broader implications. Briefly, Hackman and Oldham (1975) contend that there are three primary psychological states that significantly affect worker satisfaction:

1. Experienced meaningfulness of the work itself
2. Experienced responsibility for the work and its outcomes
3. Knowledge of results, or performance feedback

The more that work is designed to enhance these states, the more satisfying the work will be.

Positive Reinforcement—Skinner

The best way to understand the full importance of the applications of B. F. Skinner's (1953, 1971) thinking and his research results is to read his novel, *Walden Two* (1948). The book is about a utopian community designed and maintained according to Skinnerian principles of operant behavior and schedules of reinforcement. A similar application was made in an industrial situation in the Emery Air Freight case ("At Emery," 1973). By applying Skinnerian principles, which are based on numerous research findings, Emery quickly realized an annual savings of $650,000. Skinner is neither an OD practitioner nor a management consultant, but his theory and research are indeed applicable to management practices and to organizational change. For Skinner, control is key. If one can control the environment, one can then control behavior. In Skinner's approach, the more the environment is controlled the better, but the necessary element of control is the rewards, both positive and negative. This necessity is based on a fundamental of behavior that Skinner derived from his many years of research, a concept so basic that it may be a law of behavior, that people (and animals) do what they are rewarded for doing. Let us consider the principles that underlie this fundamental of behavior.

The first phase of learned behavior is called *shaping,* the process of successive approximations to reinforcement. When children are learning to walk, they are reinforced by their parents' encouraging comments or physical stroking, but this reinforcement typically follows only the behaviors that lead to effective walking. *Programmed learning,* invented by Skinner, is based on this principle. To maintain the behavior, a schedule of reinforcement is applied and, generally, the more variable the schedule is, the longer the behavior will last.

Skinner therefore advocates positive reinforcement for shaping and controlling behavior. Often, however, when we consider controlling behavior, we think of punishment ("If you don't do this, you're gonna get it!"). According to Skinner, punishment is ineffective. His stance is not based entirely on his values or whims, however. Research clearly shows that, although punishment may temporarily stop a certain behavior, negative reinforcement must be administered continuously for this certain process to be maintained. The principle is the opposite of that for positively reinforced behavior. There are two very practical concerns here. First, having to reinforce a certain behavior continuously is not very efficient. Second, although the punished behavior may be curtailed, it is unlikely that the subject will learn what to do; all that is learned is what *not* to do.

Thus, the way to control behavior according to Skinnerian theory and research is to reinforce the desirable behavior positively and, after the shaping process, to reinforce the behavior only occasionally. The implication of Skinner's work for organizations is that a premium is placed on such activities as establishing incentive systems, reducing or eliminating many of the control systems that contain inherent threats and punishments, providing feedback to all levels of employees regarding their performance, and developing programmed-learning techniques for training employees.

The application of Skinner's work to OD did not occur systematically until the 1970s. Thus, his influence is not as pervasive as is Maslow's, for example. Skinner's behavior-motivation techniques as applied to people also raise significant questions regarding ethics and values: Who exercises the control, and is the recipient aware? Thus, it is not a question of whether Skinner's methodology works, but rather how and under what circumstances it is used.

The Group as the Focus of Change—Lewin

The theorist among theorists, at least within the scope of the behavioral sciences, is Kurt Lewin. His thinking has had a more pervasive impact on organization development, both direct and indirect, than any other person's. It was Lewin who laid the groundwork for much of what we know about social change, particularly in a group and by some extrapolation in an organization.

According to Lewin (1948, 1951), behavior is a function of a person's personality, discussed primarily in terms of motivation or needs, and the situation or environment in which the person is acting. The environment is represented as a field of forces that affect the person. Thus, a person's behavior at any given moment can be predicted if we know that person's needs and if we can determine the *intensity* and *valence* (whether the force is positive or negative for the person) of the forces impinging on the person from the environment. Although Lewin borrowed the term *force* from physics, he defined the construct psychologically. Thus, one's *perception* of the environment is key, not necessarily reality. An example of a force, therefore, could be the perceived power of another person. Whether or not I will accomplish a task you want me to do is a function of the degree to which such accomplishment will respond to a need I have and how I perceive your capacity to influence me—whether you are a force in my environment (field).

Lewin made a distinction between *imposed* or induced forces, those acting on a person from the outside, and *own* forces, those directly reflecting the person's needs. The implications of this distinction are clear. Participation in determining a goal is more likely to create own forces toward accomplishing it than is a situation in which goal determination is imposed by others. When a goal is imposed on a person, his or her motives may match accomplishment of the goal, but the chances are considerably more variable or random than if the goal is determined by the person in the first place. Typically, then, for imposed or induced goals to be accomplished by a person, the one who induced them must exert continuous influence or else the person's other motives, not associated with goal accomplishment, will likely determine his or her behavior. This aspect of Lewin's theory helps to explain the generally positive consequences of participative management and consensual decision making.

Another distinction Lewin made regarding various forces in a person's environment is the one between *driving* and *restraining* forces. Borrowing yet another concept from physics, quasi-stationary equilibria, he noted that the perceived status quo in life is just that—a *perception*. In reality, albeit psychological reality, a given situation is a result of a dynamic rather than a static process. The process flows from one moment to the next, with ups and downs, and over time gives the impression of a static situation, but there actually are some forces pushing in one direction and other, counterbalancing forces that restrain movement. The level of productivity in an organization may appear static, for example, but sometimes it is pushed higher, say by supervisory pressure, and sometimes it is restrained or even diminished by a counterforce, such as a norm of the work group. *Force-field analysis* is used to identify the counterbalancing forces that determine situations.

Change from the status quo is therefore a two-step process, according to Lewin. Step 1 is to conduct a force-field analysis, and step 2 is to increase or decrease the intensity of a force or set of forces. Change can be fostered by adding to or increasing the intensity of the forces Lewin labeled *driving forces*—

those forces that push in the desired direction for change. Or change can be fostered by diminishing the opposing or restraining forces. Lewin's theory predicts that the better of these two choices is to reduce the intensity of the restraining forces. By adding forces or increasing the intensity on the driving side, a simultaneous increase would occur on the restraining side, and the overall tension for the system—whether it is a person, a group, or an organization—would intensify. The better choice, then, is to reduce the restraining forces.

This facet of Lewin's field theory helps us to determine not only the nature of change but how to accomplish it more effectively. Lewinian theory argues that it is more efficacious to direct change at the group level than at the individual level.

If one attempts to change an attitude or the behavior of an individual without attempting to change the same behavior or attitude in the group to which the individual belongs, then the individual will be a deviate and either will come under pressure from the group to get back into line or will be rejected entirely. Thus, the major leverage point for change is at the group level—for example, by modifying a group norm or standard. According to Lewin:

> As long as group standards are unchanged, the individual will resist change more strongly the farther he is to depart from group standards. If the group standard itself is changed, the resistance which is due to the relation between individual and group standard is eliminated. (1958: 210)

Adherence to Lewinian theory involves viewing the organization as a social system, with many and varied subsystems, primarily groups. We look at the behavior of people in the organization in terms of (1) whether their needs jibe with the organization's directions, usually determined by their degree of commitment; (2) the norms to which people conform and the degree of that conformity; (3) how power is exercised (induced versus own forces); and (4) the decision-making process (involvement leading to commitment).

Changing Values Through the Group—Argyris

It is not possible to place the work of Chris Argyris in one category, one theory, or one conceptual framework. He has developed a number of minitheories, whose relationship and possible overlap are not always apparent. He has always focused largely on interpersonal and group behavior, however, and he has emphasized behavioral change within a group context, along the same value lines as McGregor's (1960) Theory Y. The work described in *Management and Organizational Development* (Argyris, 1971) best illustrates this emphasis.

Argyris's early work (1962) emphasized the relationship of individual personality and organizational dynamics. To improve satisfaction in this relationship, the organization must adjust its value system toward helping its members to be more psychologically healthy, less dependent on and controlled by the organization. The individuals must become more open with their feelings, more willing to trust one another, and more internally committed to the organization's goals.

In his thinking, research, and writing during the late 1960s and early 1970s, Argyris became more clearly associated with organization development. His thrust of this period was in (1) theorizing about competent consultation, and especially about the nature of an effective intervention, and (2) operationalizing organizational change in behavioral terms by McGregor's Theory Y (Argyris, 1971). Argyris (1970) contends that, for any intervention into an organization-social system to be effective, it must generate valid information, lead to free, informed choice on the part of the client, and provide internal commitment by the client to the choices taken.

More recently, Argyris has turned his attention to the gaps in people's behavior between what they say (he calls it espoused theory) and what they do (theory in action). People may say that they believe that McGregor's Theory Y assumptions about human beings are valid, for example, but they may not act accordingly. Argyris goes on to argue that as people become more aware of these gaps between their stated beliefs and their behavior, they will be more motivated to reduce the differences, to be more consistent.

In collaboration with Don Schön, Argyris studied and elaborated the learning process involved in obtaining greater self-awareness and organizational awareness about human effectiveness (Argyris and Schön, 1978). Argyris and Schön argue that most organizations accomplish no more than "single loop learning," that problems are solved or fixed and a single loop of learning is accomplished. To improve an organization significantly and to ensure its long-term survival and renewal, however, change must occur in more fundamental ways. Although problems must be solved in a single loop, new ways of learning how to solve problems must be learned as well. Another loop is thus added to the learning cycle—what Argyris and Schön refer to as "double loop learning." This process of learning is analogous to if not the same as the way OD is sometimes defined as a planned process of change in the organization's culture—how we do things and how we relate to one another.

The Group Unconscious—Bion

Most people believe that everyone has an unconscious: Freud has clearly had an effect. Wilfred Bion believed, as others do, that there is also a group unconscious—a collective unconscious that is more than the sum of the individual unconscious. Bion gave compelling but complex arguments for this theory (Bion, 1961; Rioch, 1970).

Bion believes that every group is actually composed of two groups, the work group and the basic-assumption group; that is, every group behaves as if it were two groups, one concerned with group accomplishment and rational actions, the other concerned with activity that stems from the unconscious and is irrational. Bion did not mean simply that a group is both rational and irrational. He went far beyond this commonly accepted dichotomy.

The *work group* is the aspect of group functioning that is concerned with accomplishing what the group is composed to do, the task at hand. The work group is aware of its purpose, or at the outset knows that its initial task is to establish clarity of purpose. The work group is sure about, or quickly becomes sure about, roles and responsibilities in the group. The work group is also clearly conscious of the passage of time and the procedures and processes needed to accomplish the task.

How many times have you been a member or leader of a group that fit such a description? I suspect that it has not been very often, if ever. Bion stated that groups do not behave in this clearly rational and sensible way because there is always another group operating simultaneously—the *basic-assumption group.*

Bion theorized that all groups function according to basic assumptions, that groups operate as if certain things are inevitable. Perhaps an analogy will help to explain. In the early days of automobiles, many people made the basic assumption that no motorized vehicle could go faster than a horse, and these people acted accordingly. In fact, some of them eventually lost money because they bet heavily on their assumption. The point is that they acted as if their beliefs were true and inevitable.

There are three types of basic-assumption groups: the dependency group, the fight-flight group, and the pairing group. The *dependency* group assumes that the reason the group exists is to be protected and to be assured of providence by its leader. The group members act immaturely, childishly, and as if they know little or nothing as compared with the leader. The leader is all-powerful and wise. In the dependency group, the leader is typically idolized. We mortals are neither omnipotent nor omniscient, however, and the group members soon realize that they must seek a "new messiah." The cycle then repeats itself with a new leader.

The *fight-flight* group assumes that it must preserve itself, that its survival is at stake, so group members act accordingly. Taking action is the key to survival, as in the proverbial army command: "Do something even if it's wrong!" It is the *group* that must be preserved, so individuals may be sacrificed through fight or abandonment (flight). The leader's role in this basic-assumption group is clear: to lead the group into battle or retreat. The best leader is one who acts in a paranoid manner, assuming that "They're out to get us, gang!" Eventually and inevitably the leader will not meet all the group's demands, at which point the group panics and searches for a new leader.

In the *pairing* group the assumption is that the group's purpose is to give birth to a new messiah. The leader in this case is purely incidental, and the group must quickly get on with the business of bringing forth the new savior. Two members therefore pair off to procreate. The two may be both male, both female, or male and female, but the basic assumption is that when two people pair, the pairing is sexual in nature, even though it may take the innocent form of establishing a subcommittee. Although new life and hope may be provided, the new messiah, as with the Christian Messiah, will soon be done away with. All the basic-assumption groups behave as if the leader must be replaced or, to use Bion's more dramatic and graphic terminology, as if the leader must be crucified.

Although the work group and the basic-assumption group are functioning simultaneously, their degree of activity varies. At times the work group is predominant and at other times the basic-assumption group holds sway.

Bion was never an OD practitioner; he was a psychotherapist. His theory, however, is applicable to interventions with teams, consultation with leaders, and diagnosis of possible processes of collusion. For a direct application and extension of the latter group or organizational dynamic, see Harvey's "Abilene Paradox" (1974), an extension of Bion's theory that explains collusive behavior on the part of members of a group.

For the OD practitioner serving as a consultant to an organizational team, Bion's theory is particularly useful for diagnosing internal problems, especially those concerning team members' relationships with the leader. For example, when subordinates defer to the boss for most if not all decisions, a basic-assumption mode of dependency may be occurring, with the work group mode being submerged. Calling this process to the attention of the group may break the basic-assumption mode and help to facilitate the group's task accomplishment. An OD practitioner might intervene with a comment like, "We seem to be looking to (the boss) for practically all of our problem solutions," and follow up with a question such as, "Don't we have experience among us that we could tap into more?" Helping a work group to stay focused on its task is a way of preventing flight and another example of how to apply Bion's theory.

Participative Management—the One Best Way— Likert

Likert is best known for two concepts: the linking pin notion of management and the four-system model of organizations. He is also known for his unequivocal advocacy of participative management as the approach to be taken by managers, regardless of organizational type. Likert's method for organization development is survey feedback. We shall consider each of these concepts briefly.

Likert's (1961) idea of the linking pin originated from his desire to design organizations in a more decentralized form without eliminating the hierarchical structure. He also wanted to incorporate more opportunity for group activity, especially group decision making, in the managerial process. Thus, each manager is simultaneously a member of two groups, one in which he or she manages and is the leader and one in which he or she is a subordinate and follows the leadership of a boss. By being a member of both these hierarchical groups, the person becomes a key *link* within the vertical chain of command. This linkage manifests itself primarily in activities involving communication and resolution of conflict. The manager-subordinate, therefore, is the primary conduit for information and facilitates the resolution of conflict, by virtue of the linking position, when there are differences between the two vertically connected organizational groups. An organization chart is drawn so that groups overlap vertically rather than in the more traditional way, as separate boxes connected only by lines.

Likert (1967) described four major models or systems of organization design: the autocratic, the benevolent autocratic, the consultative, and the participative. He used seven organizational functions to describe the four models differentially: leadership, motivation, communication, interaction and influence, decision making, goal setting, and control. His "Profile of Organizational Characteristics," a diagnostic questionnaire, is organized according to these seven functions and four models. Organizational members' answers to the questionnaire provide a perceptual profile of the organization. The profile is derived from the respondents' views of how the seven functions are managed and depicts which of the four systems seems to be predominant, at least in the eyes of the respondents.

Likert not only argued that there is one best way to manage, he also espoused one best way to conduct an OD effort. His method is survey feedback; his survey instrument, the Profile of Organizational Characteristics, organizes feedback for analysis according to the four-system model of organizational management. In an OD effort, then, Likert's approach is highly data-based, but the diagnosis is largely limited to the functions he deems important. Once the survey data are collected, they are given back in profile form to organizational family units—to a boss and his or her team—as described earlier.

Although organizational change agents may be uncomfortable with Likert's one best way and may prefer an approach that is more contingent and perhaps more flexible, they can be very sure of the direction and the objectives of the change effort.

It All Depends—Lawrence and Lorsch

For an organization to operate efficiently and effectively, one person cannot do everything, and every organizational member cannot do the same thing. In any organization, therefore, there is a division of labor. Lawrence and Lorsch (1967, 1969) call this "differentiation." In an organization with many divisions, some people must provide coordination, so that what the organization does is organized in some fashion. Lawrence and Lorsch label this process "integration." Their approach is sometimes referred to as a theory of differentiation-integration. A more appropriate label, however, and the one they prefer, is *contingency theory*. They believe that how an organization should be structured and how it should be managed depend on several factors, primarily the organization's environment, or its marketplace. The central elements of the Lawrence and Lorsch contingency theory are differentiation, integration, the organization-environment interface, and the implicit contract between the employees and management.

Differentiation means dividing up tasks so that everything that needs to be done is accomplished. To determine the degree of differentiation in an organization, Lawrence and Lorsch consider four variables:

1. *Goal certainty.* Are goals clear and easily measured or ambiguous and largely qualitative?

2. *Structure.* Is the structure formal, with precise policy and procedures, or loose and flexible, with policy largely a function of current demand?

3. *Interaction.* Is there considerable interpersonal and intergroup communication and cooperation or very little?

4. *Timespan of feedback.* Do people in the organization see the results of their work quickly or does it take a long time?

The more that units within an organization differ from one another along these four dimensions, the more differentially structured the organization is. Some units may be very sure of their goals while others are not so sure, and some units may follow strict and precise work procedures while other units are still trying to formulate working procedures. It should be clear, therefore, that highly differentiated organizations are more difficult to coordinate. In a pyramidal organization, the coordination and the resolution of conflict are handled by the next higher level of management. When organizations are simultaneously highly differentiated and decentralized with respect to management, Lawrence and Lorsch argue that integrator roles are needed, that certain people must be given specific assignments for coordinating and integrating diverse functions. These people may or may not be in key decision-making positions, but they ensure that decisions are made by someone or by the appropriate group.

How should an organization be structured, differentiated, and centralized (pyramidal) or decentralized? We already know the answer: It depends. But on what does it depend? Lawrence and Lorsch argue that it depends primarily on the organization's environment, on whether the environment is complex and rapidly changing, as in the electronics industry, or relatively simple (one or two major markets) and stable (raw materials forthcoming and predictable and market likely to remain essentially the same in the foreseeable future). The more complex the environment, the more decentralized and flexible management should be. Lawrence and Lorsch's reasoning is that, the more rapidly changing the environment, the more necessary it is that the organization have people monitoring these changes, and the more they should be in a position to make decisions on the spot. When the organization's environment is not particularly complex and when conditions are relatively stable, management should be more centralized, since this way of structuring is more efficient.

Lawrence and Lorsch consider matters of conflict resolution because conflicts arise quickly and naturally in a highly differentiated organization and the management of these conflicts is critical for efficient and effective organizational functioning. Moreover, if the organization is highly differentiated and decentralized, conflict is even more likely.

Finally, how well an organization operates is also a function of the nature of the interface between management and employees. Lawrence and Lorsch recognize the importance of individual motivation and effective supervision. They tend to view motivation in terms of expectancy, believing that employees' motivation (and morale) is based on the degree to which their expectations about how they should be treated are actually met by management in the work environment.

In summary, Lawrence and Lorsch, contingency theorists, advocate no single form of organizational structure or single style of management. The structure and the style depend on the business of the organization and its environment—how variable or how stable it is.

Lawrence and Lorsch have been among the most influential theorists for OD practitioners. Considering contingencies before acting has proven to be a popular approach to OD.

The Organization as a Family—Levinson

Harry Levinson believes that an organization operates like a family, with the chief executive officer as the father. According to Levinson, all organizations "recapitulate the basic family structure in a culture." The type of organization Levinson understands best is the family-owned business, and his theory about organizations and how they operate and change has its roots in Freudian psychology (Levinson, 1972a,b).

Levinson does not look at organizations exclusively through psychoanalytical glasses, however. He is well aware that structure, the type of business, and the outside environment affect the internal behavioral dynamics of organizations. More important for Levinson's diagnosis of an organization, however, is the nature of the organization's personality (we might call it culture). He believes that an organization has a personality, just as an individual does, and that the health of an organization, like that of a person, can be determined in terms of how effectively the various parts of the personality are integrated. He refers to this process as *maintaining equilibrium.* Levinson also believes that implicit psychological contracts exist between management and employees, based on earlier experiences from family life. If the employees behave themselves (are good boys and girls), the parents (management) will reward them appropriately. Thus, the psychological contract is characterized by dependency. Note that this aspect of Levinson's theory is similar to Argyris's theory.

Continuing the psychoanalytic paradigm, Levinson theorizes that the chief executive officer represents the ego ideal for the organizational family and that this ideal, for better or for worse, motivates the kinds of people who are attracted to the organization in the first place, the interaction patterns among people in the organization, especially in matters of authority, and the kinds of people who are promoted. If a chief executive officer stays in office for a long time, the personality of the organization slowly crystallizes over the years; those who aspire to the ego ideal stay in the organization, and those who do not leave. Accordingly, Levinson believes that history is a critical factor in diagnosing an organization.

In summary, as a consultant, Levinson uses the clinical case method in diagnosis, intervenes primarily at the top of an organization, and bases his theory on psychoanalysis. In his own words:

> You've got to take into account all the factors in an organization, just as you gather all the main facts of a person's life in taking a case history. But you need a comprehensive theory like psychoanalysis to make sense of all the facts, to make it hang together in a useful way. (1972a: 126)

Summary

At the risk of oversimplification, I have summarized ten theories by categorizing them according to perspective, emphasis, and application. A summary of these factors is given in Table 3.1. Keep in mind that there is no single, all-encompassing theory for organization development. What we have are several minitheories that help us understand certain aspects of organizational behavior and OD. Taken together and comparatively, they become more useful to the practitioner who must cope with an ever-changing, complex, total organization.

Thus, OD comes from many sources and has its roots in more than one methodology and in a variety of theories and concepts. The background provided in this chapter, though varied, nevertheless has commonality. The trunk from these roots might be expressed as the attempt to improve an organization with methods that involve people and to create conditions whereby the talents of these people are used more effectively.

Table 3.1
Summary of Primary OD Theorists According to Their Perspectives, Emphases, and Applications

Perspective	Theorist	Emphasis	Application
Individual	Maslow and Herzberg	Individual needs	Career development, job enrichment
	Vroom and Lawler	Individual expectancies and values	Reward system design, performance appraisal
	Hackman and Oldham	Job satisfaction	Job and work design, job enrichment
	Skinner	Individual performance	Incentive systems, reward system design
Group	Lewin	Norms and values	Changing conformity patterns
	Argyris	Interpersonal competence and values	Training and education
	Bion	Group unconscious, psychoanalytic basis	Group behavior diagnosis
System	Likert	Management style and approach	Change to participative management
	Lawrence and Lorsch	Organizational structure	Change contingent on organizational environment
	Levinson	Organization as a family, psychoanalytic basis	Diagnosis of organization according to familial patterns

4

Organization Development as a Process of Change

Recall the definition of OD: a planned process of change in an organization's culture through the utilization of behavioral science technology and theory. The focus of this chapter is on the process of change and on utilization of theory.

Although the practice of OD may be based on portions of several theories from the behavioral sciences, as stated in the previous chapter, there is no single, all-encompassing theory of OD. This no doubt constitutes a weakness of the field, but it is not surprising, since it is a very young field, having its origins around 1960, and is based on several disciplines. Nevertheless, most practitioners agree that three models are the underlying and guiding frames of reference for any OD effort: (1) the action research model, (2) Lewin's three-step model of system change—unfreezing, moving, and refreezing, and (3) phases of planned change as delineated by Lippitt, Watson, and Westley (1958).* These models are not mutually exclusive, and all stem from the original thinking of Kurt Lewin.

Action Research

The words *action research* reverse the actual sequence (Brown, 1972). In practice, research is conducted first and then action is taken as a direct result of what the research data are interpreted to indicate. As French and Bell (1978) have pointed out,

---

*Lippitt et al.'s model is an elaboration of Lewin's three steps. Schein (1987) has provided a more recent elaboration. We shall cover his version as well.

action research came from two independent sources, one a person of action, John Collier, who was commissioner of Indian Affairs from 1933 to 1945, the other a person of research, Kurt Lewin. Collier worked to bring about change in ethnic relations and was a strong advocate of conducting research to determine the "central areas of needed action" (Collier, 1945). He coined the label action research.

Although Lewin was an academic—a scholar, theoretician, and researcher—he was just as eminent a man of action (Marrow, 1969). Moreover, he pulled it all together when he stated that there is "no action without research, and no research without action" (Lewin, 1946). Lewin and his colleagues and students conducted many action research projects in several different domains: community and racial relations, leadership, eating habits, and intergroup conflict. The action research project that is perhaps most relevant to OD was conducted by John R. P. French (a student of Lewin's and subsequently a professor at the University of Michigan) and his client, Lester Coch. Their famous study of workers' resistance to change in a pajama factory not only illustrated action research at its best but provided the theoretical basis for what we now call participative management (Coch and French, 1948).

Wendell French (1969), Frohman, Sashkin, and Kavanagh (1976), and Schein (1980) made the action research model directly applicable and relevant to the OD process. Figure 4.1 shows French's adaptation.

Lewin's Three-Step Procedure of Change

According to Lewin (1958), the first step in the process of change is *unfreezing* the present level of behavior. To reduce prejudice, for example, the unfreezing step might be catharsis (Allport, 1945) or participation in a series of sensitivity training sessions (Rubin, 1967). For organizational change, the unfreezing step might be a series of management training sessions in which the objective for change was a more participative approach (Blake et al., 1964; Shepard, 1960) or data feedback from a survey that showed serious problems in the managerial process of the organization (Bowers, 1973; Nadler, 1977).

The second step, *movement,* is to take action that will change the social system from its original level of behavior or

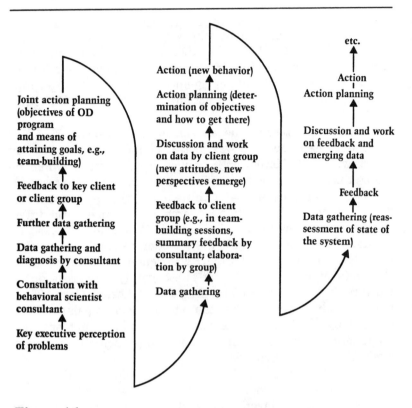

Figure 4.1
Action-Research Model for Organization Development

Source: W. L. French, "Organization Development: Objectives, Assumptions, and Strategies," © 1969 by the Regents of the University of California. Reprinted from the *California Management Review,* Volume XII, No. 2, p. 26 by permission of The Regents.

operation to a new level. This action could be organization structuring (Foltz, Harvey, and McLaughlin, 1974), team development (Beckhard and Lake, 1971), or any number of what OD practitioners call interventions.

The *refreezing* step involves establishing a process that will make the new level of behavior "relatively secure against change" (Lewin, 1958). Refreezing may include different conforming patterns, or new forms, such as collaboration rather than competition (Davis, 1967; Tannenbaum and Davis, 1969), a new approach to managing people (Marrow, Bowers, and Seashore, 1967; Seashore and Bowers, 1970), or a new reward system that will positively reinforce the desired behavior change (Lawler, 1977).

Thus, according to Lewin, bringing about lasting change means initially unlocking or unfreezing the present social system. This might require some kind of confrontation (Beckhard, 1967) or a process of reeducation. Next, behavioral movement must occur in the direction of desired change, such as a reorganization. Finally, deliberate steps must be taken to ensure that the new state of behavior remains relatively permanent. These three steps are simple to state but not simple to implement. Lippitt, Watson, and Westley (1958) and Schein and Bennis (1965; see especially Chapter 10) have helped to clarify these steps by elaborating on them.

Schein's Elaboration of Lewin's Three-Stage Model

As Schein points out: "These stages overlap and may occur very rapidly, but they are conceptually distinct, and it is important for the helper [OD practitioner] to be aware of what stage he is working in" (Schein, 1987: 93).

Stage 1. Unfreezing: Creating Motivation and Readiness to Change. Schein describes three ways of unfreezing an organization.

- Disconfirmation or lack of confirmation. Organizational members are not likely to embrace change unless they experience some *need* for it. Embracing change typically means that people are dissatisfied with the way things are—quality is below standard, costs are too high, morale is too low, or direction is unclear, for example.

- Induction of guilt or anxiety. This is a matter of establishing a gap between what is current but not working well and some future goal that would make things work better. When people recognize a gap between what *is* and what would be better and more desirable, they will be motivated via guilt or anxiety to reduce the gap. But disconfirmation and induction are not enough to accomplish the unfreezing stage, according to Schein. One more process is necessary.

- **Creation of psychological safety.** To face disconfirmation, experience guilt or anxiety, and be able to act or move, people must believe that moving will not bring them humiliation or loss of self-esteem. People must still feel worthy, psychologically safe. The consultant must therefore be concerned with people not losing face and must take care that when people admit that something is wrong they will not be punished or humiliated.

Stage 2. Changing.   This stage entails what Schein calls "cognitive restructuring," that is, helping people to see things differently and to react differently in the future. There are two main processes for accomplishing this stage.

- Identification with a new role model, mentor, boss, or consultant to "begin to see things from that other person's point of view. If we see another point of view operating in a person to whom we pay attention and respect, we can begin to imagine that point of view as something to consider for ourselves" (Schein, 1987: 105).
- Scanning the environment for new, relevant information. A brief, personal consulting example should help to clarify this point of Schein's. In working with the chairman of a company and the president or CEO, the three of us explored many reasons for their conflict with one another. To help with reducing some of this conflict, we worked hard on clarifying roles and responsibilities. In addition, I volunteered to bring to them other chairman-president/CEO models from other client organizations, some that worked very well and some that did not. This process was an activity of bringing to the two of them new, relevant information that might help them move forward with the changes needed in the relationship.

Stage 3. Refreezing. This final stage is one of helping the client integrate the changes. Schein sees this stage in two parts—self and relations with others:

- Personal refreezing is the process of taking the new, changed way of doing things and making it fit comfortably into one's total self-concept. This process involves a lot of practice—trying out new roles and behaviors, getting feedback, and making adjustments until the new way of doing things feels reasonably comfortable.

- Relational refreezing is the process of assuring that the client's new behavior will fit with significant others. In a system, when one begins to do things differently, will this difference quickly and, in any case, eventually affect others with whom the person interacts? If you and I interact frequently and I change to maintain the relationship you will have to change as well, at least to some extent to maintain the relationship. This process involves openly engaging with others about the new way of doing things, to help them see why the change is better than the old way. The process applies Stages 1 and 2 to others to get to Stage 3.

Phases of Planned Change

The Lippitt, Watson, and Westley (1958) model of planned change expands Lewin's three steps to five phases. They use the word *phase* deliberately, since *step* connotes a discrete action or event rather than the more likely reality, that step 1 has probably not been completed when step 2 is being taken, and so forth. The five phases are:

1. Development of a need for change (Lewin's unfreezing)
2. Establishment of a change relationship
3. Working toward change (moving)
4. Generalization and stabilization of change (refreezing)
5. Achieving a terminal relationship

Lippitt, Watson, and Westley viewed the change process from the perspective of the change agent. Their concept of change agent is a professional, typically a behavioral scientist, who is external or internal to the organization involved in the change process. In OD terms, this person is the OD practitioner or consultant. Lippitt and his colleagues go on to state:

> The decision to make a change may be made by the sys-
> tem itself, after experiencing pain (malfunctioning) or dis-
> covering the possibility of improvement, or by an outside
> change agent who observes the need for change in a par-
> ticular system and takes the initiative in establishing a
> helping relationship with that system. (Lippitt, Watson,
> and Westley, 1958: 10)

With respect to Phase 1, development of a need for change, Lippitt, Watson, and Westley suggest that the unfreez-ing occurs in one of three ways: (1) a change agent demonstrates the need by, for example, presenting data from interviews that indicate a serious problem exists; (2) a third party sees a need and brings the change agent and the potential client system together; or (3) the client system becomes aware of its own need and seeks consultative help.

By establishment of a change relationship, Phase 2, the authors mean the development of a collaborative working effort between the change agent and the client system. Lippitt and his colleagues make an important point when they note that "often the client system seems to be seeking assurance that the poten-tial change agent is different enough from the client system to be a real expert and yet enough like it to be thoroughly under-standable and approachable" (p. 134). Striking this balance is critical to effective consultation in OD.

Most of their elaboration on Lewin's three steps is in the mov-ing phase, or, as Lippitt and his colleagues call it, working toward change. There are three subphases to this third major phase:

1. *Clarification* or diagnosis of the client system's problem consists primarily of the change agent's collecting
   information and attempting to understand the system,
   particularly the problem areas.
2. *Examination* of alternative routes and goals involves
   establishing goals and intentions of action and also

includes determining the degree of motivation for change and the beginning of a process of focusing energy.

3. *Transformation* of intentions into actual change efforts is the *doing* part—implementing a new organization structure, conducting a specific training program, installing a new record system, and the like.

Refreezing, or the generalization and stabilization of change, is the fourth major phase. The key activity in this phase is spreading the change to other parts of the total system. This phase also includes the establishment of mechanisms or activities that will maintain the momentum that was gathered during the previous phases. Lippitt and his colleagues call this a process of institutionalization. Hornstein et al. (1971) view this as both normative and structural support for the change. Normative support means that, in the refreezing phase, organization members are conforming to new norms. To ensure this form of institutionalization, organization members must be involved in planning and implementing the action steps for change. Involvement leads to commitment—in this case, commitment to new norms. Structural support may take the form of new organizational arrangements—that is, new reporting and accountability relationships, as reflected in a new organization chart—or the placement of guardians of the new culture, the new conforming patterns. These guardians, or facilitators, of the new culture are people whose job it is (1) to monitor the state of the organization's effectiveness; (2) to see that the information that is monitored is reported to the appropriate people in the organization; (3) to provide help in understanding the information, especially in the diagnosis of problems; (4) to assist in the planning and implementation of action steps for further changes; and (5) to provide additional expertise in helping the organization to continue to change and renew where appropriate. Their primary responsibility, therefore, is to help regulate change as an organizational way of life. Hornstein and his colleagues go on to state:

> Initially, this role is typically fulfilled by an outside consultant to the organization. Frequently, he attempts to work in conjunction with some person (or persons) inside the organization. If the internal person is not trained in OD, the external consultant will usually encourage the

internal person(s) and other key individuals in the organization to develop their own resources in this area. (Hornstein et al., 1971: 352)

In other words, the more the consultant can arrange for OD-trained people to be permanent organization members, the more likely the initiated change is to last and become institutionalized as a way of life.

For the final phase, Lippitt and his colleagues argue for the achievement of a terminal relationship. What they mean is that the relationship between the change agent and the client must end. They contend that it is common for clients to become dependent on change agents and that change agents' ultimate goal is to work themselves out of a job. The underlying value of this model for change is that it creates within the client system the expertise to solve its own problems in the future, at least those problems that fall within the same universe as the original change problem.

The Generic Model for Organizational Change

The four models covered so far in this chapter—action research; Lewin's three steps of unfreezing, moving, and refreezing; Schein's elaboration of Lewin's three stages; and Lippitt, Watson, and Westley's five phases of planned change—are all part of a generic model for bringing about organizational change. This is not accidental, of course, since all four models are based on the original thinking of Kurt Lewin.

The generic model might be described as a process by which a consultant collects information about the nature of an organization (the research) and then helps the organization to change by way of a sequence of phases that involve those who are directly affected—the organization members themselves. This more general model consists of the following elements:

1. An outside consultant or change agent
2. The gathering of information (data) from the client system by the consultant for purposes of understanding more about the inherent nature of the system, determining major domains in need of change (prob-

lems), and reporting this information back to the client system so that appropriate action can be taken

3. Collaborative planning between the consultant and the client system for purposes of change (action)

4. Implementation of the planned change, which is based on valid information (data) and is conducted by the client system, with the continuing help of the consultant

5. Institutionalization of the change

To summarize and integrate the four models of change that we have considered thus far, Fig. 4.2 shows a comparison of Lewin's (1958) three steps, the action research model provided by Wendell French (1969) and Schein (1980, 1987), and Lippitt, Watson, and Westley's (1958) phases of planned change. As shown in the exhibit, the action research model for OD is the main reference point for comparison.

It should be noted that earlier thinking about planned change, especially Lippitt et al. (1958) emphasized the role of the change agent as data collector, data interpreter, feedback provider, and so on. The change agent was depicted as doing practically everything. Current practice of OD emphasizes the role of the practitioner more in terms of *facilitation,* helping the client to do many of these activities themselves (Schein, 1987). Organizational development consulting is distinct in this regard from management consulting, where the consultant usually does all of this work for the client.

Even though I have labeled this section "the generic model," it may not be. Organization change is sufficiently complex that no generic model may yet exist. In any case, it is quite appropriate to refer to another model that has been given the label of generic. The difference is that what I have called generic encompasses diagnosis and intervention whereas the one I am now referring to is labeled by its authors as a "generic model of intervention" (Bushe and Shani, 1991).

Building on the earlier work of Howard Carlson at General Motors (Miller, 1978) and Zand (1974), Bushe and Shani make the argument, with case examples to support their points, that (1) bureaucracy remains as powerful and influential

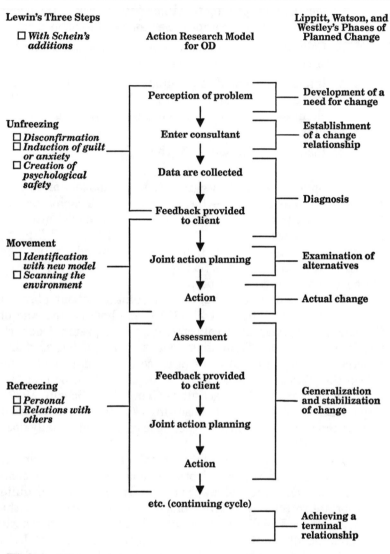

Figure 4.2
Comparison of the Four Models of Change

as ever as a primary way for organizational functioning (or non-functioning as the case may be), and therefore (2) parallel structures are required for innovation and change in large, complex bureaucracies. Galbraith (1982), using similar arguments, has also suggested alternative structures for innovation. These parallel learning structures, as Bushe and Shani refer to them, are used typically temporarily to overcome the limitations of bureaucracy. Bushe and Shani describe eight phases, which are similar to those of Kolb and Frohman (1970) and to the phases described later in this chapter.

While focusing primarily on the intervention aspect of change, these ideas of Bushe and Shani are sufficiently broad and applicable to be worthy of the label *generic*.

Now we shall consider a case that should help to understand how these models of action research, including principles applied by Bushe and Shani, and Lewin's three stages incorporating the elaborations of Schein and Lippitt et al. are applied in an actual OD consulting example.

Practicing OD: A Case History

The action research model and the phases of planned change provide the framework for OD practice. We shall consider in more specificity these practice phases, but first let us consider an actual case of OD consultation that should help our later understanding of the phases of OD practice.

I was contacted initially by Carol, the manager of human resources for a regional division of a large, international financial corporation. She reported directly to Ron, the regional manager. Carol called me because I had previously consulted with other divisions of the corporation and was therefore familiar with their business. She also told me that she had sought advice from others in the corporation and that I had been recommended. She explained that Ron was new in his position as regional manager and was anxious to make some changes. He was considering an off-site meeting with his senior management group and believed that an outside consultant might be helpful. Carol then asked if I would be interested and, if so, if we could have lunch together soon to explore the matter.

Exploration

At the lunch meeting a few days later, Carol and I asked each other many questions. She was interested in what I had done before, how I liked to work, what I might do or suggest if such-and-such were to happen, what I knew about her company's business, and whether I would be interested in continuing to consult with them if the initial effort went well. I asked her such questions as why the business had lost money four years· in a row; what Ron's predecessor was like; what Ron was like—his managerial style, his previous job history; how people in the region, especially the senior management group, felt about him, and whether any of the others thought they should have become the new regional manager instead of Ron; how the senior management group worked together—were off-site meetings common occurrences; and so forth. Toward the end of our exploratory discussion, Carol explained that she needed to talk further with Ron and that she would be in touch with me again soon.

Meeting with Ron

The following week Carol called to schedule a meeting for me with Ron. In my meeting with Ron, it was soon clear to me that he trusted Carol a great deal. He was essentially sold on me, and all we needed to do was to discuss details. He explained that, although he had been in the region for more than three years as head of consumer services, he had only been regional manager for a month. He felt pressure from higher management to make the region profitable, and he reasoned that he must have his senior management group solidly with him in order to "turn the region around." He further stated that he wanted to have an off-site meeting with his senior management group to establish two-year profit goals, to develop an overall regional business strategy, and to begin the process of building a senior management *team.*

I explained that I would like to conduct individual interviews with the members of his senior management group, including himself, determine if they thought an off-site meeting was appropriate, summarize and analyze the information from the interviews, meet with him again to go over the data, plan the meeting (if warranted), and clarify our respective roles—that he would lead the meeting and I would help. In OD language, my role would be a facilitating one.

Agreement

We reached agreement concerning what Ron wanted and how I wanted to proceed. This verbal agreement was followed a few days later with an exchange of letters to confirm our agreement in writing.

Interviews

Over a one-week period, I conducted one-hour interviews with each member of the senior management group. This group is depicted in the chart shown in Fig. 4.3. I explained to each manager that the interview would be confidential and that only a summary of the interviews in aggregate form would become public.

Although I asked many questions in each interview, I asked four general questions of everyone:

1. What are the strengths of the region?
2. What are the weaknesses of the region?
3. Are you in favor of the off-site meeting?
4. What should be the objective of the off-site meeting?

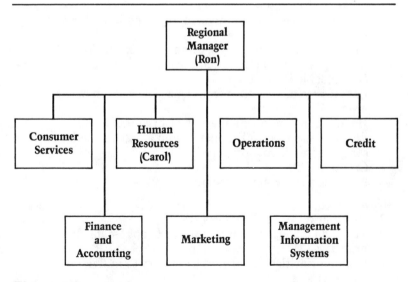

Figure 4.3
Organization Chart for Regional Division of International Financial Corporation

The interviews went well. All the managers were cooperative and expressed themselves openly and candidly, and I took many notes.

Summary and Analysis of Interviews

Although some of the managers thought the off-site meeting was somewhat premature because Ron had only been in his position for one month, others believed that the timing was right. Regardless of the timing, however, all thought an off-site meeting was a good idea. Thus, the summary of my interviews was categorized according to the three other questions—strengths and weaknesses of the regions and objectives of the off-site meeting. Table 4.1 provides a partial listing of some of the major

Table 4.1
Partial Summary of Eight Interviews Conducted with a Regional Senior Management Group

Strengths of the Region
1. Senior management group is highly experienced in the business (7)
2. Commitment of work force; community spirit (5)
3. Considerable opportunity; natural market area (3)
4. Good people throughout (3)
5. Last four years we have experienced success in many areas (3)
6. Have become more of a marketing organization (3)
7. We are technologically superior and a market leader as compared with our competitors (3)
8. Creativity (2)
9. Managers think entrepreneurially (2)

Weakness
1. Our marketing and services system (6)
2. Try to do too many things at once; do not establish priorities (3)
3. Region priorities are always secondary to individual manager's (3)
4. Lack of management depth (3)
5. Little planning (3)

(continued)

Table 4.1 *(continued)*

6. Structure (2)
7. High costs (2)
8. Overly change-oriented (2)
9. Poor reward system (2)
10. Low morale (2)
11. Internal competition (2)
12. High degree of mistrust (2)

Objectives of Off-site Meeting
1. Agree on the regional structure (7)
2. Set financial objectives for next two years (6)
3. List of things we need to do and stop doing (4)
4. Must hear from Ron about his team notions, ideas, expectations (4)
5. Some ventilation of feelings needed (3)
6. Must come together more as a top management team (3)
7. Establish standards for performance (3)
8. Increase mutual respect (2)

Note: The number in parentheses after each item indicates the number of respondents who specifically mentioned that point.

points of the interviews. As is typical for such an activity, the weaknesses listed outnumbered the strengths. People, especially managers, tend to focus more on problems than on what is going well or is positive for the organization.

Some general problems in the region became clear to me as a result of the interviews. Although the group believed that they were highly knowledgeable and experienced in their business, they recognized that remaining unprofitable was not going to get them to where they wanted to go, especially in their individual careers. There was also a conflict over whether theirs was a marketing and sales organization or a consumer services organization. Actually, it had to be both, but, from the standpoint of strategy and with respect to individuals' roles and responsibilities in lower levels of management, there was considerable ambiguity. This ambiguity contributed to problems of priorities, numbers 2 and 3 in the list of weaknesses. The emphasis on structure and financial objectives was therefore appropriate in the major objectives for the off-site meeting.

Plan for the Off-site Meeting

Ron and I met before the off-site meeting to go over my summary and analysis of the interview information and to plan the meeting. I gave him the summary and analysis of the interviews just as I would later give it to the entire group. Thus, Ron received the same information but received it earlier. The purposes of this advance notice were (1) to use the information as a basis for planning an agenda for the meeting and (2) to allow Ron to have time to understand and react to the information before the meeting. Ron would then have an opportunity to discuss his reactions to the information, particularly his feelings so that if he felt defensive, for example, he could talk about it with me and not be as defensive during the meeting. In such situations, especially if it is the first time, bosses frequently receive more criticism for problems than any other member of the group. Even if interview comments are not specifically directed at the bosses, they may feel responsible and accountable for the problems because of their positions, regardless of where the actual causes may lie. In Ron's case, he was not angry and he was not particularly defensive. He didn't think he had contributed to the weaknesses and problems any more than anyone else had. If he had been regional manager longer than a month, of course, his feelings may have been different. Ron was pleased with his group's openness and accuracy regarding the issues, and he was enthusiastic about the upcoming meeting.

Our plan for the meeting was simple and straightforward. We wanted as little interference and distraction as possible, so we would hold the meeting at a hotel-resort that was fairly remote yet comfortable. The site was less than two hours away from the region's headquarters by automobile, and it met our criteria. Regarding the agenda, we planned to begin at 4 P.M. on Wednesday. Ron would open the meeting with a statement of his goals and expectations regarding the meeting, and I would follow with a summary of the interviews. The group would then have a chance to react to and discuss the interview summary. Before dinner Ron would present some financial data that would show clearly how the region compared with the other regions (they were close to the bottom), and after some discussion we would eat dinner together as a group. Thursday morning would be devoted to setting a two-year profit goal and to establishing priorities among the many objectives. Thursday afternoon we would discuss potential obstacles to reaching the profit goal and to realizing some of the more specific objectives of the region, such as clarifying their objectives regarding the balance of marketing versus service. Friday morning we would discuss an overall strategy that would incorporate the profit goal and these objectives, and Friday afternoon would be devoted to a summary of the meeting, to members' reactions to and critique of the meeting, and to a discussion of the specific plans for follow-up.

The Off-site Meeting

The meeting proceeded essentially as planned. We took a two-hour break for lunch and some physical recreation in the middle of the day on Thursday and then worked from 2 P.M. to about 7 P.M. On Friday we had a quick lunch and continued to work until about 3 P.M., when we adjourned. This was somewhat short for such a meeting, but adequate. During the summary and critique of the meeting, I also participated, giving my observations of them as a group, and making suggestions about how they could improve their work together as a team. Everyone considered the meeting to have been worthwhile and useful, and Ron was particularly pleased. He believed that the formation of a team, as opposed to an administrative aggregate of senior managers, had begun, and I agreed.

After the Off-site Meeting

A few weeks after the meeting, Ron and I met again and agreed on a plan for my continued consultation. Some of the changes I helped to make were (1) installation of a planning function reporting directly to Ron; (2) reorganization of the consumer services area, particularly regarding the functions of marketing and sales as they related to service (an off-site meeting with the head of consumer services and his management group was part of the planning for these changes); (3) modifications in the reward and performance-appraisal processes of the region (I worked with Carol in this area); and (4) development of the senior management group into more of a team. Eventually, though certainly not overnight, the profit picture for the region began to change, and they did indeed move from the red to the black.

Now that we have the case as an illustration of OD consultation, let us reconsidser the steps I took so that we can translate the activities into OD language and understand more thoroughly the concepts and principles of this kind of consultation.

Phases of OD Practice

Based on the Lewinian concepts of unfreezing, change, and refreezing and on Lippitt, Watson, and Westley's (1958) phases of planned change, as well as Schein's (1987), but oriented more specifically to current OD practice, Kolb and Frohman (1970) give seven phases to be followed in an OD consultation: scouting, entry, diagnosis, planning, action, evaluation, and termination. I have modified their list by putting scouting and entry together, separating contracting and feedback into distinct phases, using intervention instead of action, and eliminating termination. What Kolb and Frohman call *scouting,* I call *entry,* and I consider *contracting* a more appropriate term for what they label as *entry.* Our differences are simply in labels and emphasis; the overall process is the same, except for termination, which I will explain later. Thus, my seven phases are:

1. Entry
2. Contracting
3. Diagnosis
4. Feedback
5. Planning change
6. Intervention
7. Evaluation

We shall consider each of these phases in turn, using the case to illustrate the characteristics of OD consultation.

Entry

Contact between the consultant and client is what initiates the entry phase. This contact may result from either the client's calling the consultant for an exploratory discussion about the possibility of an OD effort, as in the case example, or from the consultant's suggesting to the client that such an effort might be worthwhile. For an external consultant, the contact is likely to result from the client's initiative. For an internal consultant, either mode could occur. Internal consultants, being employees, typically feel some commitment to their organizations, or it may be part of their job descriptions to call on managers in the organization and suggest preliminary steps that might lead to an OD effort. Internal consultants also may have experienced success with organization development in one subsystem and may wish to spread this effect further within the organization. Initiating contacts with clients therefore comes naturally for internal OD practitioners, and there is certainly more opportunity for informal contacts to occur—at lunch, at committee meetings, and so forth—when questions can be asked and suggestions explored.

After the contact, the consultant and the client begin the process of *exploring* with one another the possibilities of a working relationship. The client is usually assessing whether he or she can relate well with the consultant, whether the consultant's previous experience is applicable to the present situation, and whether the consultant is competent and can be trusted.

My lunch meeting with Carol served as the beginning of the exploration process. I repeated the process with Ron, the regional manager, but this second round was rapid, since it had already been facilitated by Carol's previous meeting with and assessment of me.

During the exploration process, the consultant is assessing (1) the probability of relating well with the client, (2) the motivation and values of the client, (3) the client's readiness for change, (4) the extent of resources for supporting a change effort, and (5) potential leverage points for change—whether the client has the power to make decisions that will lead to change or whether higher authority must be sought. In my conversation with Ron, I became satisfied that he was motivated and ready for change, that he had the resources, and that he had the leverage—enough autonomy to take considerable action without getting approval from higher management.

There are additional criteria and ways of determining a client's readiness for change. Pfeiffer and Jones (1978), for example, have developed a useful fifteen-item checklist for such a determination. They urge the consultant to check, among others, such things as flexibility of top management, possible labor contract limitations (which could be crucial if job enrichment, for example, were a potential intervention), any previous experience the organization may have had with OD (or what some may have called OD, regardless of what the activities were), structural flexibility with respect to the organization's design, and the interpersonal skills of those who would be involved.

Contracting

Assuming that the mutual explorations of the consultant and the client in the entry phase progress satisfactorily, the next phase in the process is negotiating a contract. If the entry process has gone smoothly, the contracting phase is likely to be brief. The contract is essentially a statement of agreement that succinctly clarifies what the consultant agrees to do. If it is done thoroughly, the contract will also state what the client intends to do. The contract may be nothing more than a verbal agreement, with a handshake, perhaps, or it may be a formal document, with notarized signatures. Most often, the contract is considerably more informal than the latter extreme, typically involving an exchange of letters between the two parties.

Unlike other types of contracts, the OD contract states more about process than about content. According to Weisbord (1973), it is

> an explicit exchange of expectations ... which clarifies for consultant and client three critical areas:
>
> 1. What each expects to get from the relationship;
> 2. How much time each will invest, when, and at what cost;
> 3. The ground rules under which the parties will operate. (p. 1)

My contract with Ron was fairly straightforward. The letters we exchanged simply confirmed in writing what we had agreed to in our meeting. The letters summarized what I would do and some of what he planned to do. The case as I described it was indeed the implementation of our contract.

When we met after the off-site meeting, Ron and I agreed on a further contract, which was also confirmed in an exchange of letters.

It is a good practice in OD consultation to renew or renegotiate the contract periodically. In my consultation with Ron, the second contract was essentially an extension of the first, occurring about three months after the earlier one. The timing of the renewal or renegotiation is not as important as seeing that this phase is periodically repeated. It is also a good practice to have the agreement in writing. Although an exchange of letters may not necessarily constitute a legal document, the written word usually helps to avoid misunderstandings.

Diagnosis

There are two steps within the diagnostic phase: gathering information and analyzing it. Diagnosis has usually begun even at the entry phase—if the consultant is alert. How the client reacts to the possibility of change at the outset may tell a great deal not only about the client as an individual but also about the part of the organization's culture that he or she represents. Initially, therefore, information gathering is accomplished through the consultant's observations, intuitions, and feelings. Later, more systematic methods are used, such as structured interviews, questionnaires, and summaries of such organizational documents as performance records and task force reports. Once the data are collected, the consultant must then put all the varieties of information together, summarize all the information without losing critical pieces, and finally organize the information so that the client can easily understand it and be able to work with it so that appropriate action can be taken.

As we shall see in the next chapter, there are several models to help the consultant with both steps of the diagnostic phase: knowing *what* information to seek and knowing *how* to analyze and interpret the information.

In my initial work with Ron and his management group, I relied on three methods of data gathering: interviews, my observations, and my reading of two documents—one concerning Ron's thinking about long-range planning and another that summarized the issues regarding the problem of marketing versus service orientation.

My diagnosis consisted of (1) summarizing the data according to the categories of the interview questions (see Table 4.1) and elaborating on what the interviewees had said and (2) drawing certain conclusions from the combination of my observations and some relationships I perceived in the interview results.

Feedback

How effectively the consultant has summarized and analyzed the diagnostic information will determine the success of the feedback phase to a significant extent. This phase consists of holding meetings with the client system—usually first with the boss alone and then with the entire group from whom the data were collected. The size of the group would determine the number of feedback sessions to be held. If the client system consisted of a manager and his or her immediate subordinates only, then two sessions would be required, one with the manager alone and the second with the entire group, including the manager. If more than these two levels of the overall managerial hierarchy were included—for example, four levels of management, involving thirty or more people—then as many as four or five feedback sessions may be necessary. A feedback session should allow for ample discussion and debate, and a small group that does not involve multiple levels of management is best for such purposes.

A feedback session generally has three steps. First, the consultant provides a summary of the data collected and some preliminary analysis. Next, there is a general discussion in which questions of clarification are raised and answered. Finally, some time is devoted to interpretation. At this stage some changes may be made in the consultant's analysis and interpretation. Thus, the consultant works collaboratively with the client group to arrive at a final diagnosis that accurately describes the current state of the system.

In my work with Ron and his management team, I followed essentially the steps I've just outlined. The feedback phase consisted, first, of our discussion of the interview results early in the off-site meeting. Toward the end of the meeting, I provided additional feedback, which was a combination of my observations of the group as they worked together for two days and my further analysis of the interview data. I told them, for example, that I had observed that their competition with one another, a weakness some of them had identified, conformed to a particular norm. The norm seemed to be: "Let's see who among us can best identify and analyze our problems and weaknesses as a region." Everyone tackled every issue and problem, and it appeared that winning the game of "best analysis" was critical to all. My diagnosis, with which they agreed, was based in a social-psychological frame of reference and was particularly related to the concept of norm.

Planning Change

The planning phase sometimes becomes the second half of the feedback session, as happened with Ron and his team. Once the diagnosis was understood and deemed accurate, action steps were planned immediately. It has been noted that a good diagnosis determines the intervention. The only required planning may be the implementation steps—what to do. The more complex the diagnosis or the larger the client system, however, the more likely it is that the planning phase becomes a later event, following the feedback sessions. It may be best generally to allow some time to pass between feedback and planning—a few days, perhaps, but probably no more than a week. This passage of time might allow the feedback to sink in and would create an opportunity for more thought to be given to the planning process.

The purposes of this planning phase are to generate alternative steps for responding correctively to the problems identified in the diagnosis, and to decide on the step or order of steps to take. The OD practitioner again works collaboratively with the client system during this phase, primarily by helping to generate and explore the consequences of alternative action steps. The final decision of what steps to take is the client's, not the consultant's.

Intervention

The intervention phase consists of the action taken. The possibilities are numerous, and the selected interventions should be a direct reflection of and response to the diagnosis. Some examples of interventions at the individual level are job redesign and enrichment, training and management development, changes in the quality of working life, management by objectives, and career development. At the group level, interventions might include team building, the installation of autonomous work groups or quality control circles. Resolving intergroup conflict might be an intervention, as might changing such structural dimensions of the organization as reporting relationships, moving toward or away from decentalization of authority, modifying physical settings, or creating informal structures in the organization.

The interventions used in Ron's region were team building, process consultation, some minor structural changes, career development, and a change in the region's reward system by installation of a bonus plan for managers.

Whatever the intervention might be, the OD practitioner continues to work with the client system to help make the intervention successful. As Kolb and Frohman (1970) point out: "the failure of most plans lies in the unanticipated consequences of the change effort" (p. 60). The OD consultant's job is to help the client anticipate and plan for the unanticipated consequences.

Evaluation

It is usually best for someone other than the consultant to conduct an evaluation of any OD effort. The consultant cannot be totally objective, and it is difficult to concentrate on what needs changing and on evaluating its success at the same time (Lewicki and Alderfer, 1973).

The mode of evaluation may range from clients' saying that they are pleased with the outcome to a systematic research effort employing controls and multiple data analyses. A more objective and systematic evaluation is obviously better, at least for determining cause and effect. It is difficult to do a highly scientific evaluation of OD efforts. The main problem, of course, is control; it is almost impossible to have a proper control group for comparison. Furthermore, the client is usually more interested in taking action that will pay off than in objectively determining whether the action results were attributable to the OD intervention. What is important to the client is whether the action taken was successful according to the organization's usual standards—profits, reduction of costs, or higher performance in general; what *caused* the success is less important. This was essentially the case with Ron and his region, and so no formal evaluation was conducted. Evaluation did occur, however, as I periodically checked and asked for feedback, and the profit results, although they did not necessarily prove a cause-effect relationship, were sufficient evaluation in this case.

Regardless of its form or index, evaluation is very important because the process usually reinforces the change effort, and it is a primary way to learn about the consequences of our action.

In Chapters 8 and 9 we shall consider evaluation again. It should be clear that some form of evaluation is a critical part in the OD process. Although the evaluative effort does not have to meet all the standards of rigorous research and the scientific method, it must at least provide adequate data for making reasonable decisions regarding further changes.

Termination of the OD Effort

The foregoing seven phases constitute what I consider the primary, sequential actions a practitioner takes in an organization development effort. My list differs slightly in emphasis and labels from the earlier list of Kolb and Frohman (1970), but the phases are essentially the same, with one exception: Kolb and Frohman's termination phase. They argue that "the consultant-client relationship is by definition temporary" (1970: 61), that the effort either succeeds or fails. If it fails, termination is abrupt; if it is successful and the goals are reached, the consultant may not leave so abruptly, but the relationship terminates because there is no further need for consultative help. It should be noted that Kolb and Frohman's seventh step is consistent with the phases of planned change delineated earlier by Lippitt, Watson, and Westley (1958).

I do not include termination in my list of phases for three reasons. First, termination is not an applicable phase for internal OD practitioners. Although they may conclude specific programs and projects with their clients, they should not terminate the relationship. A primary role of internal practitioners is to serve as guardians of the new culture. They help to regulate the social change that has become a new routine in organizational life (Hornstein et al., 1971). This regulation may take a variety of forms, ranging from periodic checks with client managers regarding the continuing effectiveness of changes to more systematic follow-up activities, such as conducting annual surveys, attending a manager's staff meetings as a process consultant, or helping to design and conduct off-site planning or diagnostic meetings for departments or divisions.

The second reason concerns external OD consultants. A termination phase is and should be more common for external consultants than for internal ones, but it is not necessarily a requirement for effective consultation. A major goal of an external OD consultant is to see that internal resources are established for the kind of help he or she is providing. As soon as possible, internal practitioners should begin to take over the work the external consultant initiates. Thus, although the external consultant's activities with the client organization may decrease, they do not necessarily have to be terminated. Kolb and Frohman's argument for termination is to prevent the client from becoming dependent on the consultant. As an external consultant I have had long-standing relationships with some clients, but I have never felt them to be too dependent on me. Although dependency may occur as a problem in personal therapy, it rarely becomes an issue in consultation with organizations. I know of consultant-client relationships that have continued for more than a decade, and I consider them healthy and useful for both parties. An organization has a constant need for periodic, objective diagnostic check-ups by external consultants—a need that exists, incidentally, whether or not the organization's managers see it.

Finally, I do not think a termination phase is appropriate because, when OD practitioners follow the action research model, they naturally generate new data for further diagnosis and action. The process is cyclical (French, 1969), and since an organization is both dynamic and naturally follows the entropic process, there is always a great deal of consultative work to be done. For further elaboration of these three reasons, see Van Eron and Burke (1993).

Phases, Not Steps

Phases is a more appropriate term than *steps* for describing the flow of events in OD work. *Steps* implies discrete actions, while *phases* better connotes the reality of OD practice—a cycle of changes. Although it is useful for our understanding of OD practice to conceive of distinct phases, in actual practice they blend, overlap, and do not always follow one from the other. Diagnosis, for example, comes early in the OD process and intervention later, but when one is collecting information from the organization for diagnostic purposes, an intervention is occurring simultaneously; when the OD practitioner begins to ask questions about the organization and its members, he or she is intervening.

Phases is an appropriate term also because of the cyclical nature of the OD process. As the process continues, new or undisclosed data are discovered. These data affect organization members, and the members react, creating additional information for diagnosis. Further action is then planned as a consequence of the new, perhaps more refined diagnosis.

Another implication of the cyclical nature of OD relates to the characteristics of open social systems, as delineated by Katz and Kahn (1978). Two of these characteristics are relevant—the notion that organizations proceed through cycles of events over time and the notion that systems seek equilibrium. The first characteristic, that organizational life runs in cycles, is precisely the reason that OD is cyclical. Since organizations are cyclical, OD must also be in order to respond in an appropriate and timely manner. Major events in organizations—planning, budgeting, quarterly reports—are repeated over time; as these events are repeated, new data are likely to be generated each time. Two quarterly reports are rarely the same, and plans and budgets change continuously. Consequently, the diagnosis of an organization in December will be at least somewhat different from the diagnosis conducted the previous June—significantly different if a significant intervention has occurred during the intervening six months. If things in the organization are significantly different six months later, and if these differences are disturbing to organization members, they will seek equilibrium—back to the former state. Organization development involves change. When change occurs in one of the organization's components or subsystems, other subsystems act to restore the balance. Pressure is brought to bear on organizational behavior that is different from the norm of the organization's culture as it has evolved. Thus, in OD practice, for change to last, recurring diagnoses must be undertaken to determine the state of earlier interventions, and further actions (interventions) are usually needed to reinforce the new behaviors. The long-run objective is to institutionalize the change so that possibilities of changing the OD change will be resisted within the normal pattern of open-system life—equilibrium seeking.

Summary

In this chapter we have considered the four background models for any OD effort and the seven primary phases of OD consultation using a case to illustrate the phases. Although it is instructive to consider these phases—entry, contracting, diagnosis, feedback, planning change, intervention, and evaluation—as discrete steps, and although the consultative flow of events essentially follows the order of the seven phases, in practice the phases are not discrete; they blend together and overlap. When the consultant enters the client organization to collect information (by interviews, questionnaires, or observations) the intervention phase, sixth in the ordered group of seven, has already begun; and although evaluation is listed as last, it begins at the entry stage as far as the client is concerned.

These phases are therefore guides for OD consultation. They are highly useful for planning and for ordering sequences of activities and events, but they should not be considered as discrete, rigid steps to follow or as the only phases of consultation in organization development.

Finally, it should be remembered that these guides help to accomplish primary objectives of any OD effort. That is, as OD practitioners we are concerned with (1) providing people with choices, so that their feelings of freedom will not be unduly curtailed and thus their resistance will be minimized, and (2) involving people at some level of participative decision making and communication regarding the direction of organizational change, so that commitment to change implementation will be enhanced. While I have used slightly different language with this closing statement, I am meaning the same as Argyris (1970) when he describes his criteria for an effective intervention.

5

Defining the Client: A Different Perspective

During the three decades of my work in OD, I have overheard or taken part in many discussions about "Who is the client?" Is the client the head person, the boss, a particular unit or group, or the total system? In these discussions, OD practitioners have identified at least one of the above.

Let me be concrete by using an actual case, a consulting project of mine a few years ago, with a small, highly technical company, a subsidiary of a large corporation. I was introduced to the president by an employee relations person to explore the possibility of my working with the company. Contracting with the president and later with his top group went fairly smoothly. After some interviewing and observing, I was soon able to provide them with some preliminary feedback. Although the employee relations person did not accompany me during this early stage, at my request he became my internal counterpart as I began to move downward through the organization.

I looked forward to this consulting effort because I had rarely worked with an organization so small—about ninety employees—and so interesting scientifically and technically. (The firm was developing commercial lasers.) In short, this was an organization of a size that I believed I could "get my arms around" and one that seemed to be on the verge of exciting technical advances.

The top management group was relatively small, consisting of five persons including the president (see Fig. 5.1). Most of the staff was located in operations, which consisted of both manufacturing and marketing/sales. At least a third of my consulting effort was within this unit of the company.

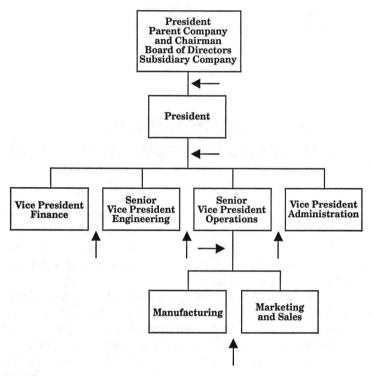

Figure 5.1
Partial Organizational Chart of Client Firm

Now to the central question: Who is my client? Answer by responding to the following multiple-choice question:
The client is:

    a. company president

    b. top management group

    c. employee relations person

    d. total company

    e. parent corporation

    f. all of the above

    g. none of the above

To be au courant, you would choose either (d) or (f). After all, OD is a total system approach to planned change that starts from the top. My contracting, however, was done first with the president and next with his immediate reports as a group. Perhaps a better answer is (a) or maybe (b). But what about the employee relations person? My coming in was originally his idea and he paved the way. Also, he later was very much involved in my efforts. Alternative (c) may be the best answer. But what about the parent company? Was I not really serving them? The president of the parent company was chairman of the board of the subsidiary. Although he was not the subsidiary's CEO, he was nevertheless clearly in a position of authority. Maybe (e) is the best reply. These answers all seem reasonable. Thus, the safest alternative should be (f).

Consider the title I chose for this chapter and now, perhaps reacting to the way I presented the multiple-choice question, you already conclude that my answer is (g). The purpose of this chapter, therefore, is to provide a rationale for that answer.

But first, one other viewpoint should be considered. Schein's (1987) definition of the client is valuable because it is practical and multiple. He states that we must think in terms of client *categories:*

- *Contact clients* approach the consultant initially (the employee relations person in my example).

- *Intermediate clients* get involved with the consultant in the early stages of the OD effort (the top management group in my example).

- *Primary clients* own a problem for which help is requested (the operations group in my example).

- *Ultimate clients* may or may not be directly involved with the OD practitioner "but their welfare and interest must be considered in planning further interventions" (Schein, 1978: 118). (In the case I described, this could be the parent company.)

The value of Schein's categories is the fact that he addresses the reality of consulting. We often do not end up where we started in the consultant-client relationship.

Relations and Interfaces

Now back to my selection of (g) "none of the above." I chose it because I believe that our client in OD consultation is never one individual, regardless of position or role, or any particular group, team, or subsystem of the organization, or any combination thereof. Even though I generally subscribe to the idea of OD being a "total system," I often wonder if changing a whole system is even possible. Besides, I have trouble defining what the total system is, since each one resides within yet a larger "total system."

The truth is that I have come to think of my client as the relationship and/or interface between individuals and units within and related to the system. Thus, the arrows in Fig. 5.1 depict my view of the true client. This in-between-ness is the main subject of my consulting.

From the perspective of the consultant role, my notion of client is not new. In his 1970 book, Argyris avoided terms such as consultant, change agent, or practitioner, favoring instead "intervenor" and "interventionist." These terms were, of course, an extension of his definition of a consultant intervention:

> To intervene is to enter into an ongoing system of relationships, to come between or among persons, groups, or objects for the purpose of helping them. There is an important implicit assumption in the definition that should be made explicit; the system exists independently of the intervenor. (Argyris, 1970: 15)

For Argyris, then, to consult is to intervene.

Margulies (1978) characterized the role of the OD consultant as a marginal one (see Chapter 8). He argued that the degree to which the consultant is effective is a function of how capable he or she is at maintaining a certain social distance between self and other individuals in the client organization and at operating on the boundaries of units rather than exclusively within them. In these ways, the consultant can more readily maintain an objective stance *in between* persons and units in conflict rather than by being *with* one or the other.

While I agree with both Argyris and Margulies regarding the consultant role, the focus here is on the other side, the client, and on the perspective of defining the client as relationships and interfaces rather than individuals and units, singular entities within the organization. To pursue this perspective, we shall first consider theory and then practice—the why and then the where and how.

Theory

Both general systems theory and the theory that underlies Gestalt therapy have furnished me with useful conceptual frameworks for understanding OD practice (Burke, 1980). Notions of entropy, input-throughput-output, and equilibrium from the former and the ideas of energy, existentialism, and polarities from the latter have been particularly helpful in understanding some mistakes I have made in consultation, that is, why some efforts turned out other than as I had expected. To explain in more depth the ideas touched on in Chapter 2, I find the theoretical thinking of Capra (1977, 1983) in high-energy physics and Prigogine (Nicolis and Prigogine, 1977) and Jantsch (1980) in chemistry and evolution, respectively, particularly stimulating, since their ideas both confirm and challenge general systems and related theory.

Capra stimulated me to consider organizational diagnosis in quite new ways. Like most OD practitioners, I have depended on models to help me make sense of all the data I collect from interviews, documents, observations, and the occasional questionnaire. I have relied on Weisbord's six boxes at certain times and on other models with clients (see Chapter 6). While they have been invaluable, they have not been the sine qua non of diagnosis. The boxes and connecting lines direct me where to look and how to interpret certain information, yet when I concentrate exclusively on the components of these models I find that I overlook other important data—the nuances, certain reappearing yet inconsistent patterns of behavior, hidden agendas, and collusions. Yes, I know it is imperative that the client organization declare its purpose and mission, clarify its strategy, design an appropriate, workable structure, provide for its members reasonable and attractive rewards, and so on (see Chapter 7). But focusing entirely on these dimensions obscures other data that should enter the consultant's field of vision. It may be that what happens out of the ordinary is just as important, if not more so, than what happens routinely. It may be that repercussions in one or more of the boxes brought about by events in another box in the model are more important for diagnosis than what happens in the changed box itself. For example, a change of leadership may have stronger implications for organizational purpose than for the organization's leadership per se.

Let us now consider some of Capra's thoughts more directly. According to Capra and other physicists, matter at the subatomic level does not exist in terms of "things" but as "probability waves." They only *tend* to exist. Those terms that we learned in high school, *protons* and *neutrons,* the subparts of an atom, are not parts, particles, or tangible things as we normally think of them. They may be conceived of as entities but only as a convenience. Capra's own words may help:

> Depending on how we look at them, they appear sometimes as particles, sometimes as waves. . . .
>
> The apparent contradiction was finally resolved in a completely unexpected way that dealt a blow to the very foundation of the mechanistic world view—the concept that matter is real. At the subatomic level, it was found, matter does not exist with certainty at definite pinpointable places but rather shows "tendencies to exist."
>
> At the atomic level, then, the solid-material objects of classical physics dissolve into wavelike patterns of probabilities. These patterns, furthermore, do not represent probabilities of things, but rather probabilities of interconnections. (Capra, 1977: 22)

Capra is therefore discussing *relations* of abstract particles. These relations constitute a unified whole. This kind of thinking suggested to me that I should consider more directly and diligently the web (to use Capra's term) of relations in organizations. It is this web, the interactions, the interfaces, that make up or at least define the total system more clearly than the units and individuals that form the connecting points. For me, this way of conceiving and diagnosing a system depicts the reality of organizational behavior more closely than other models.

Jantsch, basing much of his theorizing on the prior work of Prigogine, states that to understand the evolution of living things, one must concentrate more on disequilibrium than on equilibrium. The former, he contends, is far more natural, affirmative, and central to growth and change. To achieve equilibrium is to gain comfort, yet this victory may bring us closer to stagnation and death than to vibrancy and life. Jantsch also holds that evolution is accelerating just as the overall process of change appears to be.

His theory has been heralded by some as a paradigmatic shift comparable to Einstein's move away from Newton. Just as Einstein's theory of relativity wrested the physical sciences away from Newton's static ideas of gravity, Jantsch's ideas challenge us to view movement, relativity, and change in living systems as *constant*. He argues that all living things are always co-evolving yet maintaining a "relativity" to one another. Both Jantsch and Prigogine believe that the disequilibrium and perturbation that are from time to time in living things are actually a kind of molting, a shedding of the old within organisms as they strive to attain a higher level of existence. These perturbations, activities of disequilibrium, are signs of positive change that lead to self-organization rather than to decline. Thus, out-of-the-ordinary events may be more significant for organizational understanding than ordinary ones.

A related principle from general systems theory is the idea of the steady state and dynamic homeostasis (see Goodwin Watson's 1966 article for an analysis of resistance to change within this theoretical context). According to this principle, open systems to survive must maintain a steady state. However, a steady state is not motionless or a true equilibrium. As Katz and Kahn (1978) characterize this principle for organizations, "There is a continuous inflow of energy from the external environment and a continuous export of the products of the system, the ratio of the energy exchanges and the relations between parts, remains the same." Even though their theory contends that the steady state is not motionless, Katz and Kahn do note that "relations between parts remain the same" and they conclude that "The basic principle is the preservation of the character of the system." Perhaps their interpretation of general systems theory and Jantsch's thinking are not that different. Perhaps it is a matter of emphasis.

But it may be that practitioners of OD have overly emphasized the client's achieving a steady state and equilibrium. Yes, OD is at heart identified with change, yet one of our major interventions, team building, is more often than not a striving toward greater equilibrium. ("Let's learn to work better together; let's learn to trust; let's build a more cohesive unit"; etc.) These equilibrating goals are worthy, but if OD practitioners spend all their consulting time in this manner and in resolving conflicts, they may be helping to squash needed perturbations and disequilibrium.

Life cycle theory of organizations is pertinent to this last point (see, for example, Greiner, 1972). Usually for an organization to move successfully from one state of the cycle to another, wrenching changes have to be made even to the point of modifying the basic character of the organization.

To summarize, theory from sources other than the ones I usually turn to has challenged my way of understanding and diagnosing organizations. These ideas about matter and living things have stimulated me to concentrate more on the relationships between people and units rather than necessarily the individuals and units per se, and on unusual events rather than on routine operations.

Let me now call attention to some findings and different emphases from the world of practice that have influenced my outlook.

Practice

Some recent studies in management have further influenced my thinking about the importance of relationships and interfaces. We shall consider these studies in four different domains of relationships: the manager's relationships downward with subordinates, upward with his or her boss, lateral relationships, and the manager's unit's relationships with other individuals and units.

Managing Subordinate Relationships. There is mounting evidence that, used appropriately, a participative management approach pays off. For example, some recent research reveals that managers who move rapidly up the hierarchy tend to involve their subordinates in decision making more than do managers who move up less rapidly. These faster-rising managers were rated by themselves and their subordinates as having a participative style, whereas less successful managers were rated as having a persuasive, "selling" style or one that we might characterize as laissez-faire (Hall, 1976).

In a study of executive competence in a large federal agency, those executives who were widely considered the most competent tended to manage more collaboratively, communicate more openly, solicit information from subordinates more frequently, more often establish mutual trust and respect with subordinates, provide more opportunities for subordinates to express openly their objections and disagreements with their superior's proposed actions or decisions, and manage work group meetings in ways to ensure that a frank and open exchange of ideas occurred (Burke and Myers, 1982). There were at least sixteen other significant differences between the most competent executives and those who were less so. The six I have cited sound to me like a partial role description of a participative manager. In any case, the other behaviors were related to and supportive of the six above.

Blake and Mouton (1982) have also provided further theoretical support for their advocacy of participative management (see Chapter 6) as well as some indirect empirical evidence.

Moreover, as pointed out in a *Fortune* magazine article (Saporito, 1986), it seems quite clear now that participative management works (also, see Sashkin, 1984); what prevents this form of management becoming more pervasive in spite of the evidence, according to the magazine reporter, is managers' reluctance to share power. As one senior executive put it, "It's no fun if you *can't* make the right decisions" (p. 60).

While I believe that the overall pattern of evidence respecting executive competence leans more and more toward participative management, my point here is not to debate the issue of management style. I *do* wish to emphasize that management is becoming more and more a reciprocal process and less and less a top-down, boss-to-subordinate, one-way street. If reciprocal relationships are a crucial ingredient of management competence, then my job as a consultant is to facilitate reciprocity, to mediate a two-way street, in other words, to work *in between*.

Managing Up. We have some findings about the importance of learning how to influence one's boss. Failure to "manage up," to relate in an active rather than passive way with one's superior, can readily lead to grave problems in the organization if not outright dismissal of a subordinate. Gabarro and

Kotter (1980) advise that one should learn quickly the boss's personal and organizational goals, strengths and limitations, work habits and preferences, as well as one's own patterns and style and how they fit with the boss's. The more one knows about these subjects the more influential one is likely to be.

In the aforementioned study of federal executives, we found that three competencies in this domain are critical: the executive's (1) going to bat for subordinates with his or her superiors, (2) ability to present bad news to superiors in a constructive way, and (3) establishing good relations with upper-level executives.

OD consultants can help subordinates sharpen their abilities to influence those above them in the hierarchy. Helping subordinates to disclose threatening news, for example, will ensure that a boss is never surprised (a sin). Likewise, knowing how to deflect one's boss from his or her preferred path is no small feat, yet it is often critical to organizational effectiveness. The point, once again, is to work in between.

Managing Lateral Relationships. Another set of competencies important to federal executives is skill at managing relationships with outside contractors and with other units within their organization. Moreover, a recent intensive study of successful general managers in the private sector found that the ability and energy to maintain contact with many people (in the hundreds) in their organization was key to their effectiveness (Kotter, 1982). Successful managers knew an amazing number of people throughout the organization on a first-name basis, and they made frequent use of these relationships to be effective in their work. Maintaining a network is therefore highly significant to the success of a general manager just as it is to the politician.

What struck me about these findings is, of course, the importance of multiple relationships, of establishing as well as maintaining them. In the federal agency study, we labeled one set of the competencies (about a sixth of the total) "influence management," since they were all concerned with the executive's ability to influence others by means other than formal authority. It is perhaps in this domain of management in particular, and organizational functioning in general, that Capra's "web of relations" becomes more salient. The consultant's being able to perceive this web in all its intricacy is central to a good diagnosis and vital to constructive intervention.

Managing Unit Interfaces. In an important paper about the dilemmas of managing by participation, Kanter (1982) treats the matter of linking teams with their environment. This linkage consists of six dilemmas:

1. *Problems of turnover* ("You had to be there"). A major outcome of good team building is an increase in member participation accompanied by a lift in team spirit. This same spirit becomes a problem when new members join the team, especially if a newcomer happens to be a new boss. The boss can undercut the group's work and/or lead the team in unwanted directions. If the team is to remain effective, these new and changing relationships must be managed.

2. *The fixed decision problem.* When a group first begins to operate participatively so that a new team starts to emerge, certain ground rules, norms, and policies gradually become decisions. Later, when membership changes, the new members do not necessarily feel bound by these decisions, since they took no part in framing them. Moreover, since all team members should have influence, prior decisions should not be viewed as immutable, the new members might argue. The dilemma, then, is how to continue the process of participation yet not to be obliged continually to renegotiate the team's earlier decisions.

3. *Suboptimization:* too much team spirit. A team can become so preoccupied with itself that its members lose sight of the team's role and function within the larger organization.

4. *Stepping on toes and territories:* the problem of power. There may be other constituencies within the overall organization who believe that they have a stake in the problem or issue that the team holds as its exclusive domain. The team feels that it has worked so well together on this problem or issue that no one else is qualified to understand it as well, much less to deal with it effectively. With this knowledge and spirit comes a feeling of power that may be difficult to share when it is clear that others outside the team need to be involved.

5. *Not invented here* (NIH): the problem of *ownership* and *transfer*. It is a commonplace that individuals and organization-

al units want to do things in their own way. And the greater the team spirit, the more reluctant members may be to adopt someone else's ideas, especially another team's. This reluctance, however, may lead to the waste of "reinventing the wheel" and of not cooperating, say, in the sharing of information. Diffusion of innovation is one of the most difficult problems of organizations.

6. *"A time to live and a time to die."* Although the evidence is not yet conclusive, there is some indication that participation needs regular renewal. Members of intensive participation groups, such as quality circles and semiautonomous work teams, have experienced burnout after eighteen months of activity. Periods of interpersonal intensity should alternate with periods of distance. This suggests that some old teams need to die; new ones will form in their place. With other kinds of groups and teams, such as task forces, boards, councils, and so on, perhaps it is best to rotate membership rather than kill off old teams and start anew. Kanter's point is that it is necessary for management to find ways to sustain continuity of participation as members of groups and as units come and go.

Kanter covers other dilemmas of management participation, especially within teams themselves and in leader-member relationships. Her dilemmas concerning a team's linkage with its environment are particularly pertinent to areas of relationships and interfaces that OD practitioners may overlook. Flushed with the success of a team-building effort, the consultant may be blind to the greater need of helping the team with new members, a new leader perhaps, other units that may have a stake in some of the outcomes of the team's work, and its own team members over time, since the need for renewal will emerge sooner than one might expect.

Kanter's dilemmas of managing participation, particularly those dealing with a team and its environment, represent fertile ground for OD consultation, and further illustrate that the ground for consultation largely comprises relationships and interfaces.

Summary and Conclusions

While I have usually been clear about the person in the client organization with whom I should contract for OD consultation, I have not always been clear that my *ultimate* client was the same person, or his or her boss, or a specific organizational unit such as the top management group, or the total system. It seems to me that other OD consultants are likewise somewhat perplexed about the identity of the ultimate client. As I read works about living systems and reflect on OD practice, I conclude that my ultimate client is that *behavior* in organizations represented by *interactions,* by relationships and interfaces. These interactions represent the basic reality of organizational life and therefore my consultation should concentrate on them. Furthermore, I should pay special attention to nonroutine events of organizational life, since these occurrences generate energy among members to return the system to a steady state, to achieve homeostasis and equilibrium. It is this use of energy and its direction that will tell me more about how the organization really operates than the energy that the members of the organization expend to maintain normal, daily operations. Just as Kurt Lewin observed that the best way to diagnose an organization is to attempt to change it, we may also state that it is easier to understand an organization when it is disturbed by atypical events than when it is operating as usual.

It is not my contention that one should entirely ignore everyday routine, the organizational structure with its boxes and lines, individuals, work units, the president and the board of directors. It is more a matter of emphasis for me to focus especially on the in-between. I also believe that relationships and interfaces in organizations will grow even more important in the future because of the changing nature of authority, insofar as authority becomes more of a function of expertise and knowledge rather than position, and of the increasing degrees of complexity in managing organizations. It is virtually impossible for a single individual to know a considerable amount, much less everything, about running an organization or even a part of it. This is especially true of high-technology organizations, public or private. Thus, mutual dependency is more the rule than the exception.

Because OD practitioners are knowledgeable about interpersonal process and are skillful in dealing with relationships, there will be plenty of opportunity for constructive work, changing cultures and applying OD in new ways. We simply must become clearer about the true subject (in my term, *client*) of that work.

6

Understanding Organizations: The Process of Diagnosis

Without a framework for understanding, the data an OD practitioner collects about a client organization may remain nothing more than an array of personal comments of the who-said-what-about-whom variety. For the information to become useful, it must be treated in organizational terms. Since OD represents a systematic approach to change, and the data for diagnosis are largely in systems language, the categories for diagnosis are systems labels.

This chapter covers selected models of and theories about organizations that are useful in the diagnostic phase of OD consultation because they help to organize and systematize the potentially confusing masses of data. Among the models and theories from which the OD practitioner may choose, some are merely descriptive while others emphasize dimensions for diagnosis, thereby providing direction for change. The purpose of this chapter is to provide the practitioner with some criteria and bases for making choices.

The models and theories I have chosen to consider in this chapter are all behavior-oriented. Although some other frameworks emphasize technological, financial, or informational aspects of organizations, behavior-oriented models are more valuable for OD practice because the role of the OD practitioner is to understand what *people* do or do not do in organizations. Word processing and office technology, for example, are of interest to OD practitioners, but only in terms of the changes people will have to make, not for the electronic wizardry involved (Lodahl and Williams, 1978).

The various models we shall explore are all based on the open-system notion of input-throughput-output and all recognize that an organization exists in an environmental context and is a sociotechnical system. All recognize the same fundamentals—an open system that exists in an environment and consists of people and technology.

We shall first examine four models that are largely descriptive: a model of simplicity with structure, two models of complexity with structure, and a develop-your-own model.

Organizational Models

Weisbord's Six-Box Model

A model is useful when it helps us visualize reality, and Weisbord's (1976, 1978) model meets this criterion very well. Weisbord depicts his model as a radar screen, with "blips" that tell us about organizational highlights and issues good and bad. Just as air traffic controllers use their radar, we too must focus primarily on the screen as a whole, not on individual blips (see Fig. 6.1).

Every organization is situated within an environment and, as the arrows in the figure indicate, is influenced by and influences various elements of that environment. In Weisbord's model, the organization is represented by six boxes: purpose, structure, rewards, helpful mechanisms, relationships, and leadership. Weisbord believes that, for each box, the client organization should be diagnosed in terms of both its formal and its informal systems. A key aspect of any organizational diagnosis is the gap between the formal dimensions of an organization, such as the organization chart (the structure box), and its informal policies, such as how authority is actually exercised. The larger this gap is, the more likely it is that the organization is functioning ineffectively.

Weisbord provides key diagnostic questions for each of the six boxes. For the *purposes* box, the two most important factors are goal clarity, the extent to which organization members are clear about the organization's mission and purpose, and goal agreements, people's support of the organization's purpose. For *structure,* the primary question is whether there is an adequate fit between the purpose and the internal structure that is supposed to serve that purpose. With respect to *relationships,* Weisbord contends that three types are most important: between individuals, between units or departments that perform

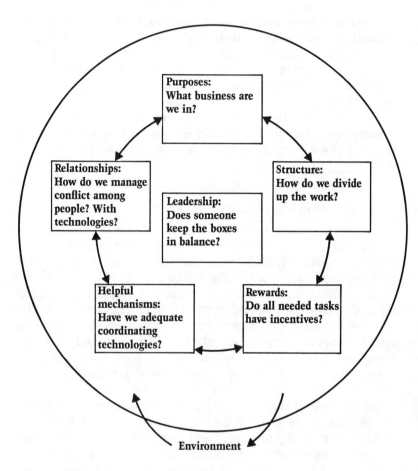

Figure 6.1
Weisbord's Six-Box Organizational Model
Source: M. R. Weisbord, "Organizational Diagnosis: Six Places to Look for
Trouble with or without a Theory," *Group and Organization Studies* 1(1976):
430–47. Reprinted by permission.

different tasks, and between the people and the nature and
requirements of their jobs. He also states that the OD consultant
should "diagnose first for required interdependence, then for
quality of relations, and finally for modes of conflict management" (Weisbord, 1976: 440).

In assessing blips for the *rewards* box, the consultant should diagnose the similarities and differences between the organization's formal rewards (the compensation package, incentive systems, and the like) and organization members' perceived rewards or punishments.

Weisbord makes the *leadership* box central because he believes that a primary job of the leader is to watch for blips among the other boxes and to maintain balance among them. To help the OD consultant in *diagnosing* the leadership box, Weisbord refers to an important book published some years ago by Selznick (1957), citing the four most important leadership tasks. According to Selznick, the consultant should determine the extent to which organizations' leaders are (1) defining purposes, (2) embodying purposes in programs, (3) defending the organization's integrity, and (4) maintaining order with respect to internal conflict.

For the last box, *helpful mechanisms,* Weisbord refers analogously to "the cement that binds an organization together to make it more than a collection of individuals with separate needs" (Weisbord, 1976: 443). Thus, helpful mechanisms are the processes that every organization must attend to in order to survive: planning, control, budgeting, and other information systems that help organization members accomplish their respective jobs and meet organizational objectives. The OD consultant's task is to determine which mechanisms (or which aspects of them) help members accomplish organizational purposes and which seem to hinder more than they help. When a helpful mechanism becomes red tape, it probably is no longer helpful.

Table 6.1 gives a summary of the six-box model and the diagnostic questions to be asked.

In summary, Weisbord's model is particularly useful when the consultant does not have as much time as would be desirable for diagnosis, when a relatively uncomplicated organizational map is needed for quick service, or when the client is unaccustomed to thinking in systems terms. In the latter case, the model helps the client to visualize his or her organization as a systemic whole without the use of strange terminology. I have also found Weisbord's model useful in supervising and guiding students in their initial OD consultations.

Table 6.1
Weisbord's Matrix for Survey Design or Data Analysis

	Formal System (Work to Be Done)	Informal System (Process of Working)
1. Purposes	Goal clarity	Goal agreement
2. Structure	Functional, program, or matrix?	How is work actually done or not done?
3. Relationships	Who should deal with whom on what?	How well do they do it? Quality of relations? Modes of conflict management?
4. Rewards (incentives)	Explicit system What is it?	Implicit, psychic rewards What do people *feel* about payoffs?
5. Leadership	What do top people manage?	How? Normative "style" of administration?
6. Helpful mechanisms	Budget system Management information (measures?) Planning Control	What are they actually used for? How do they function in practice? How are systems subverted?

Diagnostic questions may be asked on two levels:

1. How big a gap is there between formal and informal systems? (This speaks to the fit between individual and organization.)

2. How much discrepancy is there between "what is" and "what ought to be"? (This highlights the fit between organization and environment.)

Source: M. R. Weisbord, "Organizational Diagnosis: Six places to Look for Trouble with or without a Theory," *Group and Organization Studies* 1976, 1: 430–47. Reprinted by permission.

The Nadler–Tushman Congruence Model

For a more sophisticated client and when more time is available, a more complex model of organizations might be useful for OD diagnosis. In such instances, the Nadler and Tushman (1977) congruence model might serve the purpose.

Nadler and Tushman make the same assumptions as Weisbord—that an organization is an open system and therefore is influenced by its environment (inputs) and also shapes its environment to some extent by outputs. An organization thus is the transformation entity between inputs and outputs. Figure 6.2 represents the Nadler–Tushman congruence model.

Inputs.   Nadler and Tushman view inputs to the system as relatively fixed; the four they cite are the *environment,* the *resources* available to the organization, the organization's *history,* and *strategies* that are developed and evolve over time. These inputs help define how people in the organization behave, and they serve as constraints on behavior as well as opportunities for action.

As we know from the works of Burns and Stalker (1961), and Lawrence and Lorsch (1967), the extent to which an organization's environment is relatively stable or dynamic significantly affects internal operations, structure, and policy. For many organizations a very important aspect of environment is the parent system and its directives. For many organizations are subsidiaries or divisional profit centers of larger corporations, colleges within a university, or hospitals within a larger health care delivery system. These subordinate organizations may operate relatively autonomously with respect to the outside world (having their own purchasing operations, for example) but because of corporate policy may be fairly restricted in how much money they can spend. Thus, for many organizations we must think of their environments in at least two categories: the larger parent system and the rest of the outside world—government regulations, competitors, and the marketplace in general.

According to the Nadler–Tushman model, resources include capital (money, property, equipment, and so on), raw materials, technologies, people, and various intangibles, such as company name, which may have a high value in the company's market.

An organization's history is also input to the system. The history determines, for example, patterns of employee behavior,

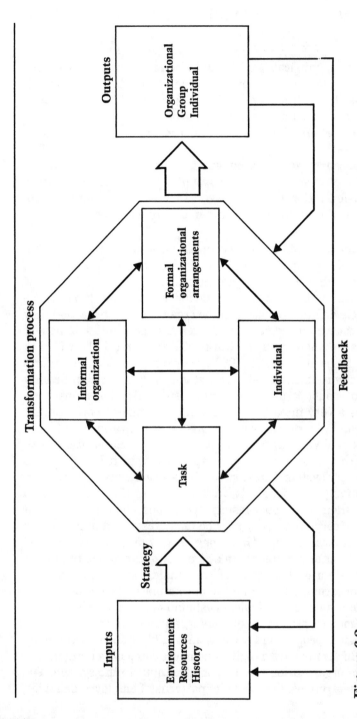

Figure 6.2
The Nadler–Tushman Congruence Model for Diagnosing Organizational Behavior

Source: D. A. Nadler and M. L. Tushman, "A Diagnostic Model for Organization Behavior," in *Perspectives on Behavior in Organizations*, edited by J. R. Hackman, E. E. Lawler, and L. W. Porter (New York: McGraw-Hill, 1977), p. 92. Reprinted by permission.

policy, the types of people the organization attracts and recruits, and even how decisions get made in a crisis.

Although strategy is categorized as an input in the models, Nadler and Tushman set it apart. Strategy is the process of determining how the organization's resources are best used within the environment for optimal organizational functioning. It is the act of identifying opportunities in the environment and determining whether the organization's resources are adequate for capitalizing on these opportunities. History plays a subtle but influential role in this strategic process.

Some organizations are very strategic; that is, they plan. Other organizations simply react to changes in their environments or act opportunistically rather than according to a long-range plan that determines which opportunities will be seized and which will be allowed to pass. As Nadler and Tushman point out, however, organizations have strategies whether they are deliberate and formal or unintentional and informal.

Outputs. We shall move to the right-hand side of the model to consider outputs before covering the transformation process. Thus we shall examine the organization's environment from the standpoint of both how it influences the system and how the organization operates internally.

For diagnostic purposes, Nadler and Tushman present four key categories of outputs: system functioning, group behavior, intergroup relations, and individual behavior and effect. With respect to the effectiveness of the system's functioning as a whole, the following three questions should elicit the necessary information:

1. How well is the organization attaining its desired goals of production, service, return on investment, and so on?
2. How well is the organization utilizing its resources?
3. How well is the organization coping with changes in its environment over time?

The remaining three outputs are more directly behavioral: how well groups or units within the organization are performing; how effectively these units communicate with one another, resolve differences, and collaborate when necessary; and how individuals behave. For this last output, individual behavior, we are interested in such matters as turnover, absenteeism, and, of course, individual job performance.

The Transformation Process. The components of the transformation process and their interactions are what we normally think of when we consider an organization—the people, the various tasks and jobs, the organization's managerial structure (the organization chart), and all the relationships of individuals, groups, and subsystems. As Fig. 6.2 shows, four interactive major components compose the transformation process that changes inputs into outputs.

The *task* component consists of the jobs to be done and the inherent characteristics of the work itself. The primary task dimensions are the extent and nature of the required interdependence between and among task performers, the level of skill needed, and the kinds of information required to perform the tasks adequately.

The *individual* component consists of all the differences and similarities among employees, particularly demographic data, skill and professional levels, and personality-attitudinal variables.

Organizational arrangements include the managerial and operational structure of the organization, work flow and design, the reward system, management information systems, and the like. These arrangements are the formal mechanisms used by management to direct and control behavior and to organize and accomplish the work to be done.

The fourth component, *informal organization,* is the social structure within the organization, including the grapevine, the organization's internal politics, and the informal authority-information structure (whom you see for what).

Congruence: The Concept of Fit. As Nadler and Tushman point out, a mere listing and description of these system inputs, outputs, and components is insufficient for modeling an organization. An organization is dynamic, never static, and the model must represent this reality, as the arrows in Fig. 6.2 do. Nadler and Tushman go beyond depicting relationships, however. Their term, *fit,* is a measure of the congruence between pairs of inputs and especially between the components of the transformation process. They contend that inconsistent fits between any pair will result in less than optimal organizational and individual performance. Nadler and Tushman's hypothesis, therefore, is that the better the fit, the more effective the organization will be.

Nadler and Tushman recommend three steps for diagnosis:

1. *Identify the system.* Is the system for diagnosis an autonomous organization, a subsidiary, a division, or a unit of some larger system? What are the boundaries of the system, its membership, its tasks, and—if it is part of a larger organization—its relationships with other units?

2. *Determine the nature of the key variables.* What are the dimensions of the inputs and components? What are the desired outputs?

3. *Diagnose the state of fits.* This is the most important step, involving two related activities: determining fits between components and diagnosing the link between the fits and the organization's outputs.

The OD consultant must concentrate on the degree to which the key components are congruent with one another. Questions such as the following should be asked:

• To what extent do the organizational arrangements fit with the requirements of the task?

• To what extent do individual skills and needs fit with task requirements, with organizational arrangements, and with the informal organization? Hackman and Oldham's (1975) job characteristics theory is a useful supplementary model for this part of the diagnosis, as is expectancy theory (Vroom, 1964; Lawler, 1973).

• To what extent do task requirements fit with both the formal and the informal organization? Information-processing models are useful supplements for this aspect of the diagnosis (Galbraith, 1977; Tushman and Nadler, 1978).

To diagnose the link between fits and outputs, the OD consultant must focus the outcome of the diagnoses of the various component fits and their behavioral consequences on the set of behaviors associated with systems outputs: goal attainment, resource utilization, and overall systems performance. Considering the component fits, or lack thereof, in light of system outputs helps identify critical problems of the organization. As these problems are addressed and changes are made, the system is then monitored through the feedback loop for purposes of evaluation.

In summary, the dimensions of the Nadler–Tushman model are quite comprehensive and have face validity. Moreover, their notion of congruence suggests certain cause-effect linkages. For example, little or no congruence between, say, strategy and structure in their model produces poor organizational performance. Also, a mismatch between what's going on in the organization's environment and strategy—for example, no plan for dealing with a recent change in government regulation—would imply a causal relationship to performance. Many other congruences or lacks thereof could be mentioned. The number of possibilities is large. Nadler and Tushman, however, do not provide ideas or, say, a formula for determining which variables in their model are central. For example, they include under a single heading, organizational arrangements, quite a number of components, any one of which could easily be central. And, finally, they do not suggest any means for knowing when congruence has occurred or what levels of congruence or incongruence produce desirable or undesirable effects.

To be fair, more recently Nadler and Tushman (1989) have had some second thoughts about their congruence position:

> While our model implies that congruence of organizational components is a desirable state it is, in fact, a double-edged sword. In the short term, congruence seems to be related to effectiveness and performance. A system with high congruence, however, can be resistant to change. It develops ways of insulating itself from outside influences and may be unable to respond to new situations. (p. 195)

Tichy's TPC Framework

With his organizational framework, Tichy (1983) focuses explicitly on the management of change. He states that there are nine organizational change levers. They are the (1) external interface, or the organization's external environment; (2) mission; (3) strategy; (4) managing organizational mission/strategy processes, that is, realistically engaging the relevant interest groups; (5) task—

change often requires new tasks; (6) prescribed *networks*—more or less, the formal organizational structure; (7) organizational processes—communicating, problem solving, and decision making; (8) people; and (9) emergent networks—more or less, the informal organization. Figure 6.3 shows how Tichy arranges

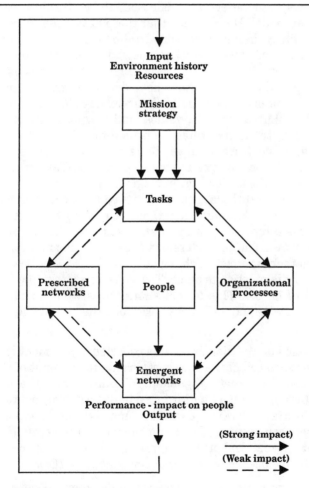

Figure 6.3
Tichy's Framework

these nine levers. He assumes that "organizational effectiveness (or output) is a function of the component of the model, as well as a function of how the components interrelate and align into a functioning system" (p. 72).

Even more important in Tichy's thinking about organization change is his TPC framework. The model in Fig. 6.3 is not unique. What makes Tichy's thinking unique is his overlay of the three systems—technical, political, and cultural—across the nine-lever model. He contends that there have been three dominant yet fairly distinct traditions guiding the practice of organization change. The *technical* view is rational, based on empiricism and the scientific method. The *political* view is based on the belief that organizations have dominant groups, and bargaining is the primary mode of change. The *cultural* view is the belief that shared symbols, values, and "cognitive schemes," as Tichy labels them, are what tie people together and form the organization's culture. Change occurs by altering norms and the cognitive schemes of organizational members. Taking only one or only two of these views for managing organizational change is dysfunctional. All three must be adjusted and realigned for successful change. The metaphor that Tichy uses to capture this thinking is a rope with three interrelated strands. The strands, or three views, can be understood separately but must be managed together for effective change.

For diagnostic purposes, Tichy uses a matrix like the one shown in Fig. 6.4. This format summarizes what he calls "the analysis of alignments." Tichy describes the use of the matrix this way:

> Based on the diagnostic data collected, a judgment is made for each cell of the matrix regarding the amount of change needed to create alignment. Working across the matrix, the alignment is within a system: technical, political, or cultural. Working down the matrix, the alignment is between systems. The 0 (no change), 1 (moderate change) or 2 (great deal of change) ratings represent the amount of change needed to align that component (p. 164).

In summary, Tichy's model includes many if not most of the critical variables important to understanding organizations. His model is unique with respect to the strategic rope metaphor and is particularly relevant to OD work, since the emphasis is on change. Moreover, Tichy is clear about what he considers to

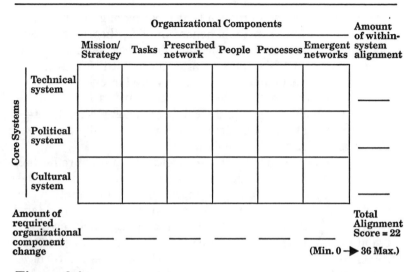

Figure 6.4
Tichy's TPC Matrix

Source: Noel M. Tichy, *Managing Strategic Change: Technical, Political, and Cultural Dynamics,* copyright © 1983 Wiley Interscience. Reprinted by permission of John Wiley & Sons, Inc.

be the primary organizational levers that must be pushed or pulled to make change happen effectively. Instead of congruence, alignment is the operational term. And Tichy provides a way of analyzing the key alignments that are necessary according to his framework. Data are first collected and then categorized within his matrix (Fig. 6.4).

There is a human component in Tichy's model, but for the most part his framework ignores issues at the individual level. He admits this omission at the end of his book by stating that he skimmed over the psychological aspects of change. The political and cultural strands are, of course, people concerns but much broader than, say, job-person match (or alignment) and local work unit activities such as teamwork. Finally, the criticism of too much congruence potentially working against change could also apply to Tichy's insistence on alignments.

Hornstein and Tichy's Emergent Pragmatic Model

The emergent pragmatic model of organizational diagnosis (Hornstein and Tichy, 1973; Tichy, Hornstein, and Nisberg,

1977) is based on the premise that most managers and consultants "carry around in their heads" implicit theories or models about organizational behavior and about how human systems actually operate. These notions are usually intuitive, ill-formed, and difficult to articulate. Because they are largely intuitive, different observers and members of organizations have different theories, which gives rise to conflicts among consultants or between consultants and clients about what is really wrong with the organization and how to fix it.

Hornstein and Tichy have developed a procedure for helping managers articulate and conceptualize their implicit models. The procedure has managers represent the information they would seek in diagnosing an organization by selecting labels from among twenty-two samples or creating their own from twenty-eight blank labels provided. The labels include such items as informal groupings, fiscal characteristics, turnover, goals, and satisfaction of members with their jobs.

Hornstein and Tichy's approach to organizational diagnosis is shared between consultant and client and among members of the client organization. The approach is called an emergent-pragmatic theory because "the model *emerges* from an exploration of both the consultant's and client's assumptions about behavior and organizations . . . and draws on both the consultant's and client's organizational *experiences* as well as on empirical and theoretical work in the field" (Tichy, Hornstein, and Nisberg, 1977: 367; emphasis added).

Another of Hornstein and Tichy's premises is that, consciously or not, organizational consultants tend to impose their theories and models of human systems on their clients. These impositions often do not fit with the client members' perceptions and beliefs or do not jibe with the client organization's underlying values. To improve congruence, Hornstein and Tichy advocate a highly collaborative approach between consultants and clients, one that results in an emergent model representing different perspectives and experiences.

There are five phases to the emergent-pragmatic approach. The consultant guides the client group through these phases:

1. Exploring and developing a diagnostic model
2. Developing change strategies
3. Developing change techniques

4. Assessing the necessary conditions for assuring success

5. Evaluating the change strategies

To summarize, the emergent-pragmatic approach to organizational diagnosis is based on the assumption that most managers and consultants have intuitive theories about how organizations function, rather than well-formed conceptual frameworks, and the assumption that many consultants impose their models and theories on client organizations, regardless of how appropriate they may be for the particular client. Hornstein and Tichy advocate a collaborative model of diagnosis to avoid the potential negative consequences of operating on the basis of these two assumptions.

The three models described earlier—Weisbord's six-box model, the Nadler–Tushman congruence model, and Tichy's TPC framework—are generic frameworks and do not fall prey to the problems of Hornstein and Tichy's two premises. When the consultant and the client do not find the Weisbord, Nadler–Tushman, or other formal models to their liking, however, the emergent-pragmatic approach offers a clear alternative. It is a do-it-yourself model and, if both consultant and client are willing to spend the time required to do it right, a mutually satisfying and appropriate model for the client organization is likely to result.

The four models described may all be categorized as *contingency* models. They do not specify directions for change prior to diagnosis; rather, what needs to be changed emanates from the diagnosis. None of the models advocates a particular design for an organization's internal structure, a certain style of behavior, or a specific approach to management. The inventors of these models do have biases, however. Weisbord says the boxes should be in balance, Nadler and Tushman argue that the various dimensions of their model should fit with one another, as does Tichy, and Hornstein and Tichy state that the consultant and client should collaborate toward the emergence of a model that is appropriate for the given organization. These biases have more to do with the best way to diagnose than with the most important dimension to change.

We now shift from organizational frameworks to more theoretical ways of describing, understanding, and changing organizations.

Lawrence and Lorsch's Contingency Theory

Lawrence and Lorsch, early contingency theorists, specify neither a best way to diagnose nor a particular direction for change. They do emphasize structure and intergroup relationships.

Lawrence and Lorsch hypothesize a cause-and-effect relationship between how well an organization's internal structure matches environmental demands and how well the organization performs (accomplishes its goals and objectives). Their research in the 1960s provided support for their argument (Lawrence and Lorsch, 1967).

To understand the use of Lawrence and Lorsch's contingency theory for diagnosis, keep in mind that its primary concepts are differentiation and integration. These two concepts represent the paradox of any organization design—that labor must simultaneously be divided and coordinated or integrated. Within the Lawrence and Lorsch framework and for diagnostic purposes, therefore, we want to examine our client organization along the dimensions they consider to be important. The methodological appendix of their book provides considerable detail concerning these dimensions and the questions to ask for obtaining the relevant information (Lawrence and Lorsch, 1967). The following lists summarize these dimensions and some of the related questions.

Environmental Demands

1. On what basis does a customer evaluate and choose between competing suppliers in this industry (price, quality, delivery, service, and so forth)?
2. What are the major problems an organization encounters when competing in this industry?
3. Have there been significant changes in the market or technical conditions in this industry in recent years?

Differentiation

1. Regarding structure, what is the average span of control? How important is it to have formal rules for routing procedures and operations?
2. Regarding the time span of feedback, how long does it take for employees to see the results of their perfor-

mance? (In sales, for example, the time lag is typically short, whereas in R&D it may take years.)

3. Regarding interpersonal relationships, how important are they, and how much interaction is necessary?
4. Regarding goal certainty, how clear-cut are the goals? How are they measured?

Integration

1. How interdependent are any two units: high (each depends on the other for survival), medium (each needs some things from the other), or low (each functions fairly autonomously)?
2. What is the quality of relations between units?

Conflict Management

1. What mode of conflict resolution is used: forcing (top-down edicts), smoothing (being kind and avoiding), or confronting (exposing differences and solving problems)?
2. How much influence do employees have on the hierarchy for solving problems and making decisions?

Employee-Management Contract

1. To what extent do employees feel that what is expected of them is appropriate?
2. To what extent do employees feel that they are compensated and rewarded fairly for their performance?

Summary. These five dimensions represent the organizational domains that Lawrence and Lorsch believe most important for effective diagnosis. Based on their research findings, the organizational diagnostician would be looking for the degree of match between environmental demands and complexities and the internal organizational structure. The greater the environmental complexity, the more complex the internal design should be. If the organization's markets change rapidly and are difficult to predict and forecast, and if the environment in general fluctuates considerably, the organization's internal structure should be relatively decentralized so that many employees can be in touch with the environment and can act quickly as changes occur. Under these conditions, differentiation may still be high, but a premium is placed on integration. There must be sufficient integrating mechanisms so that communication flows adequately across and among the many subunits and so that superiors in the hierarchy are kept well informed. The plastics industry represented this type of organization in the Lawrence and Lorsch research study. When the environment is relatively stable and not particularly complex (the container industry in their study), a fairly simple and straightforward internal structure may be best, with functional division of labor and centralized authority.

The issue is not whether one organization should be highly differentiated and another highly integrated but that they should be highly differentiated *and* integrated. High integration seems to be important regardless of environment, and differentiation may be lower for organizations with stable environments. The paradox remains in any case: Both are needed, but they are antagonistic—the more the organization is differentiated, the more integration is required.

The organizational diagnostician should also seek the mode of conflict resolution. Lawrence and Lorsch found that the more organization members and units confront their differences and work to resolve them, rather than smoothing them over or squashing them with edicts from on high, the more effective the organization tended to be.

Finally, it is necessary to know the degree of employees' satisfaction with their psychological contract with the organization. There is apparently a positive relationship between clarity of employees' understanding of what is expected of them—their perceived satisfaction with the rewards they receive for performance—and overall organizational performance.

Although Lawrence and Lorsch are contingency theorists, particularly with respect to organization structure, they too have their biases. They stress interfaces—between the organization and its environment, between and among units within the organization, and between individual employees and the organization as represented by management.

Normative Theories

Unlike contingency theorists, normative theorists argue that, for organization development, there is one best way to and direction for change. Major proponents of normative theory are Likert (1967) and Blake and Mouton (1968, 1978).

Likert's Profiles

Likert categorizes organizations, or systems in his terms, as one of four types:

System 1. Autocratic, top-down, exploitative management

System 2. Benevolent autocracy (still top-down but not as exploitive)

System 3. Consultative (employees are consulted about problems and decisions but management still makes the final decisions)

System 4. Participative management (key policy decisions are made in groups by consensus)

Likert's approach to organizational diagnosis is standardized. The mode used is a questionnaire, the "Profile of Organizational Characteristics," with six sections: leadership, motivation, communication, decisions, goals, and control. (The latest version is labeled the "Survey of Organizations.") Organization members answer questions in each of these sections by placing the letter N at the place on a twenty-point scale that best represents their opinion now and a P at the place that indicates their previous opinion—how they experienced their organization one or two years ago. Sometimes the consultant asks organization members to use an I instead of a P, to indicate what they would consider ideal for each of the questions.

Organizational profiles typically fall into the System 2 or System 3 categories. If the ideal response is used, its profile will usually occur to the right of the now profile, toward or within System 4. In such cases, the direction for change is established, toward System 4.

When one declares that there is one best way, in this case System 4 management, others usually demand evidence. Is System 4 management a better way to run an organization than System 3 or 2 or 1? Contingency theorists, of course, would say no; it depends on the type of business, the nature of the environment, and the technology involved. Likert contends that, regardless of these contingencies, System 4 is best. Likert's (1967) own research supports his claim, and so does research by others. A longitudinal study of perhaps the most systematic change to System 4 management—conducted in the Harwood-Weldon Company, a manufacturer of sleepwear—is a noteworthy example (Marrow, Bowers, and Seashore, 1967). Changes were made in all dimensions of Likert's profile as well as in work flow and organizational structure. The durability of these changes was supported by a later study conducted by Seashore and Bowers (1970).

A System 4 approach was also used as the change goal for a General Motors assembly plant (Dowling, 1975). As a result of these deliberate change efforts toward System 4, significant improvements were accomplished on several indices, including operating efficiency, costs, and grievances.

In summary, Likert's approach to organizational diagnosis is structured and directional. It is structured by use of his questionnaire and later versions of his profile (Taylor and Bowers, 1972), and it is directional in that data that are collected are compared with System 4. The survey feedback method (see Chapter 3 and Mann, 1957) is used as the main intervention; that is, the data from the questionnaire (survey) are reported back to organizational members in a set manner.

In order to use Likert's approach, the consultant should feel comfortable with the questionnaire method as the primary mode for data gathering and with System 4 management as the goal for change. Although participative management may feel comfortable as a change goal for many consultants and clients, the relatively limited diagnosis by profile characteristics only may not be so comfortable.

Blake and Mouton's Grid Organization Development

The other normative approach to OD is based on the managerial grid model developed by Blake and Mouton (1964, 1978). Like Likert's System 4 approach, the grid method of OD is structured and involves a high degree of packaging. Blake and Mouton also argue that there is one best way to manage an organization. Their label is 9,9, which also represents a participative style of management.

Blake and Mouton also depend on questionnaires, but grid OD (Blake and Mouton, 1968) goes far beyond an initial diagnosis with a questionnaire. Blake and Mouton start from an initial, general diagnosis. In a cross-cultural study of what managers consider the most common barriers to business effectiveness and corporate excellence, Blake and Mouton (1968) found that communication topped the list of ten, and a lack of planning was second. These two barriers were selected by managers much more frequently than the remaining eight (74 percent noted communication and 62 percent mentioned planning); morale and coordination, for example, the next most frequently mentioned barriers, were noted by less than 50 percent. Blake and Mouton further pointed out that communication and planning were the top two mentioned regardless of country, company, or characteristics of the managers reporting. These two major barriers, and the other less prevalent ones, are symptoms of organizational problems, not causes, according to Blake and Mouton. The causes lie deeper in the system. Faulty planning, for example, is a result of an organization's not having a strategy or having a strategy that is based on unsound rationale. Communication problems derive from the nature of the supervision practiced in the organization.

For addressing these underlying causes, Blake and Mouton have developed a six-phase approach to organization development that considers both the organization's strategic plan, or lack thereof, and the style or approach to supervision or management. They contend that, to achieve excellence, an organizational strategic model should be developed and the supervisory style should be changed in the direction of participative management. Organization members should first examine managerial behavior and style and then move on to develop and implement an ideal strategic organizational model. Before explaining the six phases of their OD approach in more detail, we should consider Blake and Mouton's managerial style model, the Managerial Grid®, because most of their normative rationale is based on this model.

Building on earlier research work on leadership, in which the dual functions of a leader were variously labeled as initiation of structure and consideration, task and maintenance, and task and socioemotional behaviors, Blake and Mouton (1964) simplified the language by using terms closer to managers' understanding: *production* and *people*. They did more, however; the creative aspect of their work was to conceptualize each of the two leader functions on a continuum, one for the manager's degree of concern for production and one for his or her concern for people, and to put the two together in the form of a graph, a two-dimensional model.

Blake and Mouton (1981) contend that they have done more than merely simplify the language and create nine-point scales. They argue that the original dimensions—initiation of structure and consideration—and those that followed, especially Hersey and Blanchard's situational leadership model, were conceptualized as independent dimensions. Blake and Mouton's dimensions—production and people—are interdependent, however, and represent attitudes more than behavior. They note that leadership is not possible without both task and people. We shall now consider Blake and Mouton's model in more detail.

Any manager will have some degree of concern for accomplishing the organization's purpose of producing products or services—that is, a concern for production, results, or profits. A manager will also have some degree of concern for the people who are involved in helping to accomplish the organization's purpose. Managers may differ in how concerned they are with each of these managerial functions, but how these two concerns mesh for a given manager determines his or her *style* or approach to management and defines that manager's use of power.

Blake and Mouton chose nine-point scales to depict their model and to rank the manager's degree of concern for production and people; 1 represents a low concern and 9 indicates a high concern. Although there are eighty-one possible combination, Blake and Mouton realistically chose to consider only the four more or less extreme positions, represented in the four corners of the grid, and the middle-of-the-road style, position 5,5 in the middle of the grid. Figure 6.5 illustrates the managerial grid and defines each of the five primary styles.

As noted earlier, Blake and Mouton contend that communication problems in the organization stem from the nature of supervision. The predominant style in U.S. organizations today can be characterized as 5,5 (Blake and Mouton, 1978). A popular book at the time, *The Gamesman* (Maccoby, 1976), was a description of Blake and Mouton's 5,5 manager. In an unpub-

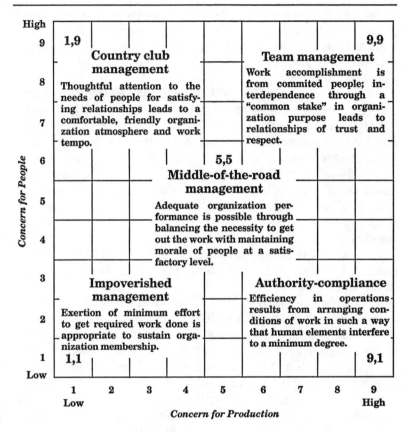

Figure 6.5
The Leadership Grid® Figure

Source: The Leadership Grid® Figure from *Leadership Dilemmas–Grid Solutions,* by Robert R. Blake and Anne Adams McCanse (formerly the Managerial Grid Figure by Robert R. Blake and Jane S. Mouton) Houston: Gulf Publishing Company, p. 29. Copyright © 1991, by Scientific Methods, Inc. Reproduced by permission of the owners.

lished study a colleague, Barry Render, and I also found 5,5 to be the predominant style of middle managers in a large government agency ($N = 400$). This style, according to Blake and Mouton, is bureaucratic and mechanistic, thus less than effective, especially regarding communication. The three styles labeled 9,1, 1,9, and 1,1 are even poorer, causing similar if not worse communication problems. The 9,9 style, then, is best when practiced consistently and will assure significantly fewer problems of communication. Training managers to adopt a 9,9 style will therefore lead to significantly fewer barriers to organizational effectiveness.

The six phases of Grid Organization Development begin with a one-week seminar at which participants assess their present styles and learn the behaviors associated with the 9,9 style. Participants also receive feedback on their styles from their fellow group members.

Phase 2 of grid OD is teamwork development. Assessment again takes place, to identify the norms and working characteristics of all managerial teams in the organization, starting with the top team and moving downward in the hierarchy to include the others.

Phase 3 is intergroup development. The objective of this phase is to reduce win-lose patterns of behavior between groups in the organization.

Phase 4 is development of an ideal strategic corporate model. Essentially what is called corporate strategic planning, this phase begins with the development of an ideal strategic organization, usually done by the top management team.

Phase 5 is implementation of the ideal strategic model. This phase, similar to what Beckhard and Harris (1977) later called transition management, consists of moving toward the ideal model in a carefully managed, evolutionary manner while continuing to run the organization as before.

Phase 6 is systematic critique. During this final phase, the change effort is evaluated and so-called drag factors are identified. (*Drag* factors are specific barriers that still exist and must now be overcome.)

Phases 1–3 are thus designed to deal with communication barriers to organizational effectiveness, and Phases 4–6 deal with the planning barriers.

It is interesting that not until Phase 6 do Blake and Mouton begin to deal with an organization diagnostically in terms like those of the other diagnostic models we have considered. Blake and Mouton have evidently decided that all fairly large organizations that are not already involved in OD have serious communication and planning barriers to effectiveness. These two primary barriers must be reduced first, and grid OD will do the job. At Phase 6 we will see how effectively the first five phases have progressed and we will know, in particular and in detail, what barriers must now be tackled.

Blake and Mouton never state it, but they apparently assume that, unless an organization learns how to communicate more effectively (practice 9,9 management) and plan more logically and systematically (build an ideal strategic model and begin to implement it), its management will never be able to deal optimally with the specifics of running a business. Phase 6 in the grid OD sequence gets to the specifics.

Levinson's Clinical-Historical Approach

Levinson's theory of organization behavior is grounded in psychoanalytic theory and views organizations in familial dimensions: "An organization is composed of persons in authority and 'siblings' who relate to these authorities" (Levinson, 1972a: 23). Because it is so closely aligned with psychoanalytic theory, it is not surprising that Levinson's approach to organizational diagnosis (1972b) is very detailed, emphasizes history, and generally relies on clinical methods. Using this approach, the consultant does a workup on a client organization much as a physician would do with a patient and obtains as complete a history as possible, especially in terms of how the organization fits into its environment. In the search of information, Levinson suggests:

> Most newspapers have morgues, or files of clippings, filed by subject. Historical societies often have much information on file. Large organizations will frequently be the subject of articles in trade or professional magazines which may be located through libraries.... The sheer availability of various kinds of information is a datum of diagnostic value. (p. 26)

Just as physicians "take a history," order a blood test, and thump the patient's body here and there, Levinson also stresses observation. He notes: "Since the consultant is his own most important instrument, he should begin [by using] his antennae for sensing subtleties" (p. 18). Levinson suggests that the consultant request a tour of as much of the organization as time and practicalities permit in order to form and record initial impressions. "The consultant will find it helpful to keep a diary of his experiences in the company, to record events and observations which will not likely be reported in interviews or questionnaires" (p. 19).

Levinson (1972a) relies on six categories of data for diagnosis.

1. Consultant observations and feelings. Notes on how the consultant experiences the organization, especially initial impressions, are recorded and become a set of information for later diagnosis.

2. Factual data. Recorded policies and procedures, historical data on file in the organization, annual reports, job descriptions, personnel statistics, and former consultant or task force reports are perused. Collecting this information is not enough, according to Levinson; analyzing how the data interrelate is important, as is the type of language used. The language will convey attitudes toward people and assumptions about what motivates employees.

3. Outside information. Information is collected, primarily through interviews, from the organization's suppliers and competitors, cooperating organizations, agents, professional associations, and the like. This information will help the consultant understand the organization's environment in general and the impact it has on the client.

4. Pattern of organization. The organization chart and the authority-responsibility structure of the organization are the primary indicators of patterns of organization. Levinson stresses a holistic approach rather than a view of the interaction of just one or two subsystems.

5. Settings. According to Levinson, "First overall organizational purposes and then how these purposes are subdivided into specific functions performed by definable groups within definable temporal and physical space.... The consultant must learn where and by whom essential functions of the organization are carried out" (1972a: 28). Levinson also notes in this context what Rice (1958) has called the time dimension: "temporal boundaries within which the setting's central purpose is accomplished ... such as factory shift work ... or ... planning activities in a management group" (Levinson, 1972a: 29).

6. Task patterns. Group-level variables exist in each setting. Levinson cites four such patterns.

Complementary activities—contributions of each work group member toward some common goal

Parallel activities—group members performing essentially identical tasks

Sequential activities—group members performing some phase of the overall group task

Individualized activities—unique functions performed by each person

These patterns constitute a setting, and the consultant attempts to learn the setting boundaries by analyzing the task patterns.

It is important to note that, although Levinson's theoretical base is psychological and his method of diagnosis is patterned after the clinical model, he does not become absorbed in pieces of the system. His approach is systemic and holistic. Although he is biased toward a Freudian view, he does not lose himself in the analytics but rather looks for systemic issues and considers how the organization influences and is influenced by its environment, how subparts of the organization relate, and how work flows from one setting, activity, and function to another. Thus, being an organizational diagnostician of the Levinson school would require a thorough grounding in psychoanalytic theory, an understanding of the clinical method of diagnosis, and a systems view of organizations that highlights patterns of relationships and work flow.

Summary

In this chapter we have considered the diagnostic phase of organization development consultation in some depth by examining certain models. These models—Weisbord's six-box model, Nadler and Tushman's congruence model, Tichy's TPC framework, Hornstein and Tichy's emergent-pragmatic model, Lawrence and Lorsch's contingency model, the normative models of Likert and Blake and Mouton, and Levinson's historical-clinical approach—are not the only ones available (see next chapter, for example). For OD purposes, however, they are some of the most relevant ones and they demonstrate the diversity of the field. There is considerable choice for the OD practitioner-consultant.

I do not often have the time required for using Levinson's approach, although I like his thoroughness and the systemic-flow perspective. When time is short and my client is naive about systems, Weisbord's six-box model works well. Nadler and Tushman's model is appealing for some of the same reasons Levinson's is, but it is easier to work with and easier to communicate to a client. Tichy's framework is fairly easy to understand, yet somewhat complex in use. Hornstein and Tichy's approach is very useful for clients who are concerned that a consultant might impose something on them, and it is useful for setting the stage for in-depth diagnosis. Lawrence and Lorsch's contingency model is currently the most popular one among OD practitioners, and with good reason. It emphasizes organizational structure, which was overlooked by OD people in the early days, and shows how the organization's environment has an internal impact. Likert's and Blake and Mouton's theories are appealing because they clearly show the way, but if their approaches are chosen, they must be followed completely; a partial application will not work. Their high degree of structure and their normative view turns away some OD practitioners. Under certain circumstances, however, I have found both to be useful—Likert's profile for providing an outside, more objective questionnaire assessment of an organization, and Blake and Mouton's grid for providing a framework for examining managerial style in the organization.

An OD practitioner's choice from among these models should be based primarily on two considerations. First, it is difficult to use a model effectively if one does not understand it. Second, the practitioner should feel comfortable with the model and its approach. If one does not really believe in participative management, using Likert's or Blake and Mouton's approach is not likely to be successful, for example.

As the following chapter shows, I have my own model. As the chapter also shows, my colleague George Litwin and I have tried to learn from many of the models and theories that have preceded ours.

7

The Burke–Litwin Model of Organizational Performance and Change*

In presenting this causal model (therefore a normative view, Burke and Litwin, 1992) I am attempting to provide yet another perspective, and at the same time demonstrate that this more recent framework captures some of the best qualities of previous models. As does Tichy in the TPC framework, this model takes certain positions about organization change and thus *predicts* behavior and performance consequences and therefore deals with cause (organizational conditions) and effect (resultant performance).

Important background regarding the development of the model (the concepts of organizational climate and culture) will be presented first, followed by a description of the model. Finally, suggestions for ways to use the model as well as case examples will be provided.

Background

Climate. The original thinking underlying the model came from George Litwin and others during the 1960s. In 1967 the Harvard Business School sponsored a conference on organizational climate. Results of this conference were subsequently published in two books (Litwin and Stringer, 1968; Tagiuri and

---

*This chapter is based in part on Burke and Litwin (1989).

Litwin, 1968). The concept of organizational climate that emerged from this series of studies and papers was that of a psychological state strongly affected by organizational conditions, such as systems, structure, and managerial behavior. In their theory paper, Tagiuri and Litwin (1968) emphasized that there could be no universal set of dimensions or properties for organizational climate. They argued that one could describe climate along different dimensions, depending on the kind of organization being studied and the aspects of human behavior involved. They described climate as a molar, synthetic, or changeable construct. Further, the kind of climate construct they described was relatively malleable; it could be modified by managerial behavior and by systems and strongly influenced by more enduring group norms and values.

This early research and theory development regarding organizational climate clearly linked psychological and organizational variables in a cause-effect model that was empirically testable. Using the model, Litwin and Stringer (1968) were able to predict and to control the motivational and performance consequences of various organizational climates established in their research experiment.

Culture. The concept of organizational culture is drawn from anthropology and is used to describe the relatively enduring set of values and norms that underlie a social system. These may not be entirely conscious. Rather, they constitute a "meaning system" that allows members of a social system to attribute meaning and value to the variety of external and internal events they experience. Such underlying values and meaning systems change only as continued culture is applied to generations of individuals in that social system.

The distinction between climate and culture must be very explicit because this model attempts to describe both climate and culture in terms of their interactions with other organizational variables. Thus this model builds on earlier research and theory with regard to predicting motivation and performance effects.

In addition, the variables that influence and are influenced by climate need to be distinguished from those influenced by culture. Thus there are two distinct sets of organizational dynamics. One set primarily is associated with the transactional level of human behavior or the everyday interactions and exchanges that create the climate. The second set of dynamics is concerned with processes of human transformation; that is, sudden "leaps" in behavior; these transformational processes are required for genuine change in the culture of an organization. Efforts to distinguish transactional and transformational dynamics in organizations have been influenced by the writings of James McGregor Burns (1978) and by consultants' efforts to change organizations.

The Model

The Burke–Litwin model has been refined through a series of studies directed by Burke (Bernstein and Burke, 1989; Fox, 1990; Michela et al., 1988). Recent collaboration has led to the current form of this model, which attempts

1. to specify the interrelationships of organizational variables; and

2. to distinguish transformational and transactional dynamics in organizational behavior and change.

Figure 7.1 summarizes the model.

In accordance with accepted thinking about organizations from general systems theory (Katz and Kahn, 1978), the external environment box represents the input and the individual and organizational performance box represents the output. Feedback loops go in both directions. The remaining boxes of the model represent the throughput aspect of general systems theory.

The model is complex, as is the rich intricacy of organizational phenomena. However, this model, exhibited two dimensionally, is still an oversimplification; a hologram would be a better representation.

Arrows in both directions convey the open-systems principle that change in one factor will eventually have an impact on the others. Moreover, if the model could be diagrammed so that the arrows were circular (as they would be in a hologram), reality could be represented more accurately. Yet this is a *causal* model. For example, although culture and systems affect one

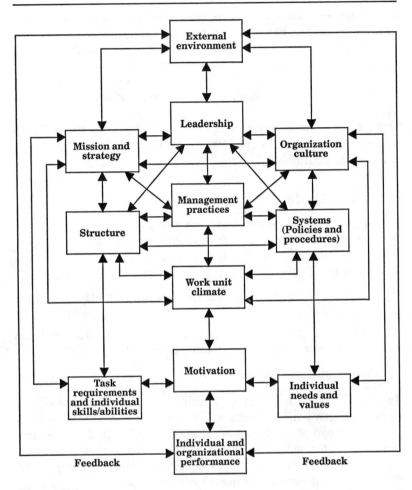

Figure 7.1
The Burke–Litwin Model of Organizational Performance and Change

Source: The Burke-Litwin Model of Individual and Organizational Performance.
Copyright © 1992, W. Warner Burke Associates, Inc.

another, culture has a stronger influence on systems than vice versa.

The model could be displayed differently. External environment could be on the left and performance on the right, with all throughput boxes in between, as with the Nadler–Tushman model (see Chapter 6). However, displaying it as shown makes a statement about organizational change: Organizational change stems more from environmental impact than from any other factor. Moreover, with respect to organizational change, the variables of strategy, leadership, and culture have more "weight" than the variables of structure, management practices, and systems; that is, having leaders communicate the new strategy is not sufficient for effective change. Changing culture must be planned as well as aligned with strategy and leader behavior. How the model is displayed does not dictate where change could start; however, it does indicate the weighting of change dynamics. The reader can think of the model in terms of gravity, with the push toward performance being in the weighted order displayed in Fig. 7.1.

In summary, the model, as shown in Fig. 7.1, portrays the following:

- The primary variables that need to be considered in any attempt to predict and explain the total behavioral output of an organization
- The most important interactions among these variables
- The ways the variables affect change

Transformational and Transactional Dynamics

The concept of transformational change in organizations is suggested by such writers as Bass (1985), Burke (1986), Burns (1978), McClelland (1975), and Tichy and Devanna (1986). Figure 7.2 displays the transformational variables (the upper half of the model). *Transformational* refers to areas in which alteration is likely caused by interaction with environmental forces (both within and without) and which require entirely new behavior sets on the part of organizational members.

Figure 7.3 shows the transactional variables (the lower half of the model). These variables are very similar to those originally isolated by Litwin and Stringer (1968) and later by Michela et al. (1988). They are *transactional* in that alteration occurs primarily via relatively short-term reciprocity among people and groups. In other words, "You do this for me and I'll do that for you."

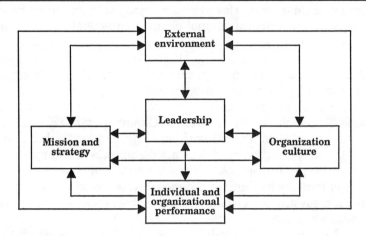

Figure 7.2
The Transformational Factors

Each category or box in the model can be described as follows:

External environment. Any outside condition or situation that influences the performance of the organization. These conditions include such things as marketplaces, world financial conditions, political/governmental circumstances, and so on.

Mission and strategy. What employees believe is the central purpose of the organization and how the organization intends to achieve that purpose over an extended time.

Leadership. Executive behavior that provides direction and encourages others to take needed action. For purposes of data gathering, this box includes perceptions of executive practices and values.

Culture. "The way we do things around here." Culture is the collection of overt and covert rules, values, and principles that guide organizational behavior and that have been strongly influenced by history, custom, and practice.

Structure. The arrangement of functions and people into specific areas and levels of responsibility, decision-making

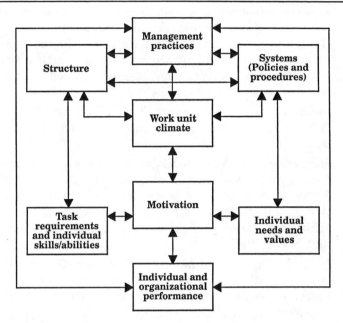

Figure 7.3
The Transactional Factors

authority, and relationships. Structure assures effective implementation of the organization's mission and strategy.

Management practices. What managers do in the normal course of events to use the human and material resources at their disposal to carry out the organization's strategy.

Systems. Standardized policies and mechanisms that are designed to facilitate work. Systems primarily manifest themselves in the organization's reward systems and in control systems such as the organization's management information system, goal and budget development, and human resource allocation.

Climate. The collective current impressions, expectations, and feelings of the members of local work units. These in turn affect members' relations with supervisors, with one another, and with other units.

Task requirements and individual skills/abilities. The behavior required for task effectiveness, including specific skills and knowledge required for people to accomplish the work assigned and for which they feel directly responsible. This box concerns what is often referred to as job-person match.

Individual needs and values. The specific psychological factors that provide desire and worth for individual actions or thoughts.

Motivation. Aroused behavioral tendencies to move toward goals, take needed action, and persist until satisfaction is attained. This is the net resultant motivation; that is, the resultant net energy generated by the sum of achievement, power, affection, discovery, and other important human motives.

Individual and organizational performance. The outcomes or results, with indicators of effort and achievement. Such indicators might include productivity, customer or staff satisfaction, profit, and service quality.

Climate Results from Transactions; Culture Change Requires Transformation

In the causal model, day-to-day climate is a result of transactions related to issues such as

- *Sense of direction.* The effect of mission clarity, or lack thereof, on one's daily responsibilities.
- *Role and responsibility.* The effect of structure, reinforced by managerial practice.
- *Standards and commitment.* The effect of managerial practice, reinforced by culture.
- *Fairness of rewards.* The effect of systems, reinforced by managerial practice.
- *Focus on customer* versus internal pressures or standards of excellence. The effect of culture, reinforced by other variables.

In contrast, the concept of organizational culture has to do with those underlying values and meaning systems that are difficult to manage, to alter, and even to be realized completely (Schein, 1992). Moreover, instant change in culture seems to be a contradiction in terms. By definition, those things that can be changed quickly are not the underlying reward systems but the behaviors that are attached to the meaning systems. It is relatively easy to alter superficial human behavior; it is undoubtedly quite difficult to alter something unconscious that is hidden in symbols and mythology and that functions as the fabric helping an organization to remain together, intact, and viable. To change something so deeply embedded in organizational life does indeed require transformational experiences and events.

Using the Model: Data Gathering and Analysis

Distinguishing transformational and transactional thinking about organizations has implications for planning organizational change. Unless one is conducting an overall organizational diagnosis, preliminary interviews will result in enough information to construct a fairly targeted survey. Survey targets would be determined from the interviews and, most likely, would be focused on either transformational or transactional issues. Transformational issues call for a survey that probes mission and strategy, leadership, culture, and performance. Transactional issues need a focus on structure, systems, management practices, climate, and performance. Other transactional probes might involve motivation, including task requirements (job-person match) and individual needs and values. For example, parts or all of "The Job Diagnostic Survey" (Hackman and Oldham, 1980) might be appropriate.

An OD consultant helping to manage change would conduct preliminary interviews with, say, fifteen to thirty representative individuals in the organization. If a summary of these interviews revealed that significant organizational change was needed, additional data would be collected related to the top or transformational part of Fig. 7.1. Note that in major organizational change, transformational variables represent the primary levers, those areas in which change must be focused. The following examples represent transformational change (concentrated at the top of the model, as illustrated in Fig. 7.2).

1. An acquisition in which the acquired organization's culture, leadership, and business strategy are dramatically different from those of the acquiring organization (even if both organizations are in the same industry),

thereby necessitating a new, merged organization (for an example of how the model has been used to facilitate a merger, see Burke and Jackson, 1991)

2. A federal agency in which the mission has been modified and the structure and leadership changed significantly, yet the culture remains in the past

3. A high-tech firm whose leadership has changed recently and is perceived negatively, whose strategy is unclear, and whose internal politics have moved from minimal (before) to predominant (after). The hue and cry here is "We have no direction from our leaders and no culture to guide our behavior in the meantime."

For an organization in which the presenting problem is more a fine-tuning or improving process, the second layer of the model (shown in Fig. 7.3) serves as the point of concentration. Examples include changes in the organization's structure; modification of the reward system; management development (perhaps in the form of a program that concentrates on behavioral practices); or the administration of a climate survey to measure job stratification, job clarity, degree of teamwork, and so on.

It is also useful to consider the model in a vertical manner. For example, Bernstein and Burke (1989) examined the causal chain of culture, management practices, and climate in a large manufacturing organization. In this case, feedback to executives showed how and to what degree cultural variables influenced management practices and, in turn, work-unit climate (the dependent variable).

The change effort at British Airways (BA) is a good example of an organization in which practically all boxes of the Burke–Litwin model were eventually examined and changed. The model provided a framework for executives and managers in BA to understand the massive change they were attempting to manage. To understand the model in use a bit more as well as to consider a significant example of large system change, let us review the change in BA.

Change at British Airways

Prior to 1987 and practically since World War II (although two organizations for most of that time period), British Airways (BA) was a government organization, the product of a merger between British European Airways (BEA) and British Overseas Airways Corporation (BOAC) in the early 1970s. These two organizations had in turn been spawned from Britain's Royal Air Force. The BA of 1983, when Colin Marshall arrived as president and CEO, operated largely as a function of its history, rather like the military, and was draining the British treasury with financial losses year after year. Moreover, passengers referred to BA as "bloody awful." Prime Minister Margaret Thatcher had decided earlier that BA was to be privatized and had brought in Lord John King, a successful businessman, to be chairman. King recruited Marshall from Avis Rent-A-Car in 1983 and gave him the charge and the authority to change BA so that it could survive privatization.

In addition to the external environmental force on British Airways by Prime Minister Thatcher and her government administration, another key environmental change was the growing deregulation of international air traffic—many air fares were no longer set by governments but instead by the marketplace.

Internally, BA had to change its mission and strategy as well as its corporate culture. BA's mission was to serve with distinction as the United Kingdom's flagship airline and strategically to compete both domestically and internationally. The mission and strategy would need to change more toward the customer and BA would need to become much more competitive. The culture would need to be transformed from one described as bureaucratic and militaristic to one that was service oriented and market driven.

Let us now consider the changes that took place in BA's mission and strategy, leadership, and culture, in other words the transformational changes.

Mission and Strategy. To make BA more competitive and to reduce costs, the first step Marshall took was to reduce the size of the workforce from about 59,000 to 37,000. The downsizing was done with a certain amount of compassion via primarily early retirements with substantial financial settlements. Marshall's background was marketing in a service industry and he began to change BA's strategy accordingly. BA was to become "The World's Favourite Airline" with a strong emphasis on the customer by providing superior service.

Leadership. Of course the major change here was the hiring of Marshall. He in turn hired Nicholas Georgiades, a psychologist and former professor and consultant, as head of human resources. Georgiades developed the specific tactics and programs required to bring about the culture change. Gordon Dunlop led the way financially via his position as chief financial officer. He was indispensable in transforming the accounting and financial functions from a government orientation to one that helped managers to understand competition and the marketplace.

Culture. Led by Georgiades, a series of programs and activities were developed to shift the culture from too much bureaucracy to a real service orientation. The first program was called "Putting People First." "Aimed at helping line workers and managers understand the service nature of the airline industry, it was intended to challenge the prevailing wisdom about how things were to be done at BA" (Goodstein and Burke, 1991: 12).

The next steps were to focus even more intensely on the culture. Georgiades conceptualized the process metaphorically as a "three-legged stool." The seat was the new, desired culture (customer-service oriented) and the three legs were (1) the "Managing People First" (MPF) program, a five-day residential experience to help managers learn about how to manage their people in such a way (more participatively, for example) that they would be more service oriented; (2) performance appraisal where half of a manager's evaluation was based on results and half on *how* the results were achieved, the how being an incorporation of the behaviors and practices emphasized in the MPF program; and (3) pay for performance, rewarding managers according to how they were rated in (2) above.

In addition to these interventions primarily targeted at management, a five-day residential training program was conducted for all human resource people in BA. This program concentrated on consultation skills to enhance the HR people's abilities to help line managers to apply what they had learned in the MPF program.

Part of the rationale for concentrating on managers in the early stages of the culture change was based on the research work of Ben Schneider. In a series of studies (Schneider, 1980, 1990; Schneider and Bowen, 1985) he has demonstrated that how "front line" people in a service business (in his case, banks; therefore, tellers, loan officers) are treated by their respective supervisors has a differential effect on customer satisfaction. In bank branches where front-line employees were managed more participatively as opposed to bureaucratically—following procedures strictly, for example—customer satisfaction was significantly higher. With British Airways being a service business, we applied this same principle. You do not have to teach cabin crew members or ticket agents how to smile. Rather you need to teach managers about how to manage these front-line people so that smiles come naturally by their desire to treat customers with respect and enthusiasm. The MPF program was therefore designed and conducted to help managers to manage more participatively, openly, respectfully, enthusiastically, and with greater trust in their subordinates. Managers cannot manage the myriad of hour-by-hour contacts that employees who have direct contact with customers encounter every day, those 50,000 "moments of truth" as Jan Carlzon, another successful airline CEO, described in his popular book (Carlzon, 1987). Managers can, however, work with their subordinates in an involving manner that will in turn have a positive effect on customers.

In summary, since the BA change was clearly fundamental and transformational in nature, concentrating on the top three boxes of the Burke–Litwin model that were changed in response to external environment demands was the appropriate approach to take. Subsequently, efforts were concentrated on (1) the climate via team-building processes, (2) support systems by modifying, for example, rewards (pay for performance) and, as noted above, (3) training all human resource people in consulting skills to help managers apply what they had learned in the MPF program.

For a more detailed description of the history behind the BA change and a brief overview of the change effort, see the case by Leahey and Kotter (1990). Goodstein and Burke (1991) have provided a more comprehensive analysis of the change process itself at BA.

That BA has changed is now a matter of record (Goodstein and Burke, 1991). It is one of the most profitable airlines in the world and its significantly improved service means that now passengers consider it "bloody awesome" rather than "bloody awful" (see *Business Week,* October 9, 1989: 97).

Considering the Burke–Litwin model from a vertical perspective entails hypothesizing causal effects and assuming that the "weight" of change is top-down; that is, the heaviest or most influential organizational dimensions for change are external environment, first and foremost, and then mission-strategy, leadership, and culture.

It is interesting to note that executives and managers typically concern themselves with the left side of the model illustrated in Fig. 7.1: mission and strategy, structure, task requirements and individual skills or abilities. In contrast, behavioral scientists are more likely to be concerned with the right side and middle of Fig. 7.1: leadership, culture, systems (especially rewards), management practices, climate, individual needs and values, and motivation. For a fundamental, large system change effort one should be concerned with the entire model and with a more effective integration of purpose and practice.

As with other models, the Burke–Litwin model has its limitations. For example, the model does not explicitly account for technology, the organization's technical strengths, those core competencies that make it competitive in the marketplace, or effective in accomplishing its mission. Since technology largely pervades the entire organization, displaying the Burke–Litwin model three-dimensionally with technology as the third dimension might improve its validity.

Conclusion

Provided we do not allow ourselves to be trapped by a particular model, and as a consequence "not see" certain, critical information about an organization, using a model for diagnosis is highly beneficial. A sufficiently comprehensive model can help us to organize data into useful categories and to see more easily and quickly domains in the organization that need attention. Choosing the model should depend on at least three criteria. First, the model should be one that you as a practitioner thoroughly understand and feel comfortable with as you work with organizational members. Second, the model you choose should fit the client organization as closely as possible; that is, be comprehensive enough to cover as many aspects of the organization as appropriate, yet be simple and clear enough for organizational members to grasp fairly quickly. Third, the model should be one sufficiently comprehensive to allow you to gather your data about the organization according to the model's parameters without missing key bits of information.

8

Planning and Managing Change

It is easy to write, if not to assume, that diagnosis is one activity and intervention (that is, planning and implementing change) is quite another. In practice, however, this is simply not true. As Schein (1969) pointed out, simply entering a human system to conduct a diagnosis is an intervention.

It is helpful to our understanding, nevertheless, to consider the phases of planning and managing change as following diagnosis and feedback. Thus, once a diagnosis has been made and feedback has been provided to the client, it is time to plan the appropriate steps to take so that problems identified in the diagnostic phase are addressed and a more ideal future state for the organization can be determined. Guiding this planning phase should be a set of coherent and interrelated concepts—a theory, model, a conceptual frame of reference.

This chapter first defines intervention and then covers the planning and management of change phase in more detail. Finally, we shall consider ways to determine if progress is being made in a change effort.

According to Argyris (1970), collecting data from an organization is intervening, which supports Schein's contention and our earlier claim that the phases of OD are not discrete. For this phase of organization development, however, we shall think in terms of some specified activity, some event or planned sequence of events that occurs as a result of diagnosis and feedback. The process of moving from a functional way of organizing to a project form, for example, regardless of how long it takes (and it might take months) could constitute an OD intervention. Another example of a possible OD intervention would be a singular event and would take a comparatively short period of time. Either type of activity could serve as an OD intervention, provided the event responds to an actual and felt need for change on the part of the client, involves the client in the planning and implementing of the change (intervention), and leads to change in the organization's culture.

Criteria for Effective Intervention

Argyris (1970) has specified similar criteria for what he considers the primary tasks of an interventionist (OD practitioner). His three criteria are (1) valid and useful information, (2) free choice, and (3) internal commitment. By *valid and useful information,* he means "that which describes the factors plus their interrelationships, that create the problem for the client system" (p. 17). According to Argyris, the information the OD practitioner has collected from and about the client accurately reflects what people in the organization perceive and feel, what they consider to be their primary concerns and issues, what they experience as complexities and perhaps accompanying frustrations of living within and being a part of the client system, and what they would like to see changed. Argyris goes on to specify that, if several independent diagnoses lead to the same intervention, the data the practitioner has gathered are valid.

For all practical purposes this first task of an interventionist, obtaining valid and useful information, is similar to my first criterion for intervention, responding to an actual and felt need for change on the part of the client. If valid information is obtained by the practitioner, it will reflect a need. If the practitioner responds to that need, he or she will have done so by providing valid and useful information.

By *free choice,* Argyris means that "the locus of decision making [is] in the client system" (p. 19) and that the client is provided alternatives for action. No particular or specified action is automatic, preordained, or imposed.

By *internal commitment,* Argyris means that the client owns the choice made and feels responsible for implementing it. Organization members act on their choice because it responds to needs, both individual and on behalf of the organization.

The primary tasks of choice and internal commitment will be accomplished if the practitioner involves the client in planning and implementing the intervention. Argyris does not specify cultural change, my third criterion. He implies that, if the practitioner accomplishes the three primary tasks, the organization's culture will be changed. This is only an implication, however; he does not specify it.

Although there are similarities between Argyris's criteria and mine, the primary difference is that I am expressing processes or means while he is stating end states or outcomes. Either way of expressing these criteria makes sense.

Planning the Intervention or Change

We may or may not agree on the fine points concerning a definition of and the criteria for an effective intervention. Unless there is some readiness for change within the client organization, definitions and criteria are no more than an academic exercise. I have heard Richard Beckhard express it one way and Harry Levinson another, but both essentially said, when it comes to organization (or individual for that matter) change: "No pain, no change." Unless enough key people in the organization feel a real need for change, none is likely to occur, at least none that is planned and managed.

The initiation of change, I should point out, is typically in response to changes in the organization's external environment, as was Prime Minister Thatcher's decision to privatize British Airways. In other words, it is rarely true that top management comes together and states "Why don't we change the organization?" More likely, top management in initiating change is doing so as a reaction to changes in the organization's marketplace, to changes in technology, to changes in government regulations, to stronger competition, and so forth.

Readiness for Change

Sometimes determining readiness is quite obvious and straightforward. The company's sales have fallen dramatically, costs have risen so sharply that profit doesn't exist anymore, turnover and absenteeism are significantly out of line when compared with others in the same industry, morale has never been lower or the market strategy doesn't seem to work anymore—these are some obvious and rather straightforward examples of a need for change. Under any of these circumstances, it is not difficult to determine a readiness. As was the case for British Airways (Chapter 7), the need for change was extremely clear. The degree of readiness varied among BA employees, but the need was obvious. In other instances, or even in the instances listed above, everyone may not see or understand a need for change. In this situation, the need must be generated. This may be done in either of two ways. One way is to gather information, the facts, about the current situation and contrast this information with where the organization was supposed to have been by this time. In other words, it is a matter of comparing actual achievements with what was desired, the organization's goals or mission.

Assuming that organizational members identified with these goals (no minor assumption, I should emphasize) and they then see a significant difference between actual and desired, they will experience a need to reduce the difference or gap between actual and what is desired. In this case, the desired state is known; not known is how far off the mark the organization's actual performance is from that which is desired. Contrasting actual with desired creates the required motivation for change.

Another way to generate a need for change is to develop a more desirable future state. Organizational members may be satisfied with the status quo and experience no need for change unless and until they are presented with a possibility of something better, more desirable. It might mean a lot of hard work and a considerable modification in the way that work is done, but the new mission and differences in how work would be accomplished may be sufficiently attractive that a motivational pull toward this more desirable future state would be generated. This, of course, requires leadership.

Even though generating a need for change may be accomplished in either of these two different ways, the principle is the same. Presenting people with a discrepancy between what is and what is desired will create tension, and the motivation will be in the direction of reducing that tension, that is, to move toward the more desired state. This principle of human behavior is based on sound theory and research; see, for example, Lewin (1936) or Duvall and Wicklund (1972).

Preparing the client for change, what we have labeled readiness, is what Lewin called the unfreezing stage (see

Chapter 4). Unfreezing is creating conditions whereby the client is shaken loose (unfrozen) from the status quo. The client's mental and emotional set has been broken and the client is therefore more amenable to consider, if not accept, change. For more elaboration on this stage, as well as additions to our understanding of Lewin's next two stages, changing and refreezing, see Schein (1980) and Chapter 4.

We have also used the terms *actual* and *desired* state. This is the language of Beckhard and Harris (1977). Developing a new mission, a new vision, a fresh image of the future is the process of creating a desired state, a way of being, of working that is more desirable than the present state. Planning any change effort involves this kind of development—that is, creating an image of the more desired future state. This creative process is not easy to do. Even more difficult, however, is moving the organization to that desired future. Beckhard and Harris (1977), based on the earlier thinking of Lewin, view the change process in three "states":

Present State → Transition State → Future State

While determining the future state is obviously critical, Beckhard and Harris concern themselves far more with the transition state, managing the change process, the more difficult phase.

Hanna (1988) has added to the Beckhard and Harris transition state by emphasizing in his coverage of managing change the importance of

- Developing a true commitment to the change
- Training in the requisite skills
- Dedicating sufficient resources
- Overcoming old habits, and
- Managing the environment

Power and Leadership

In addition to determining readiness and preparing the client organization for change by contrasting actual with desired, other planning activities need to occur. It is a leadership function to see to it that the future state is developed. Leaders in the organization need to be far more concerned with determining the future than specifying how to get there. Gaining commitment from organizational members to the future state, a plan, is critical; gaining commitment to implementing the plan, as Hanna has emphasized, is even more critical. More will be stated on this latter point in the next section.

A leadership function, therefore, is to make certain that a plan for the future is in place, that the plan is adequately communicated, and then to generate energy within the organization to support the transition.

In any sizable organization formal as well as informal leaders exist. Often overlooked in a change effort is the latter group. It is obvious that senior management needs to be "on board." If unionized, leaders within the union(s) need to be involved and supportive. All of the key managers who head the various boxes on the organization chart need to be on board. Not so obvious, however, are those who informally, from time to time, influence people's opinions. In an organization such as the National Aeronautics and Space Administration, for example, informal leadership comes from scientists and engineers who are not line, operational administrators but who are, as individuals, highly respected. Their opinions about matters are sought and they are influential. If these highly respected, listened-to, powerful individuals are not supportive of the change effort, resistance among organizational members will be greater than would otherwise be the case. It is wise, therefore, early in the planning process, to engage these informal leaders in discussing what change is needed and what is more desirable for the future.

Also informal and powerful indeed is the political process, a process that is typically subterranean, below the surface, not discussed openly much less in formal meetings within the organization (see Tichy's TPC framework, Chapter 6). By *political* I mean those activities and processes in an organization that emanate from one's self-interest, or the particular interest of a group, that may not be in the overall interest of the organization. Typically when faced with the possibility of organizational change, organizational members rarely at the outset ask the question, "What is the plan for the future?" but instead, whether openly or not, they ask "How will the change affect me?"

It is not a matter of right versus wrong. It is more a simple matter of human nature. Thus, during the planning phase, it is imperative to address these political concerns, motivated by self-interest. That is, it is imperative to respond to the tacit question, "What's in it for me?" Some examples of the advantages to be provided by the future state might be these:

- A mission and purpose that is more meaningful and inspiring
- A set of goals and objectives that are not only clearer but more sensible in potential for attainment as well
- A more participative, pleasant place to work
- A reward system that is more flexible and responsive to individual differences
- A more decentralized structure that supports greater worker autonomy as well as responsiveness to the customer
- A management information system that handles relevant, current, and therefore, useful data
- A set of management practices that engender trust

With such examples, a statement of the future could begin to be responsive to individuals' personal concerns. More specificity regarding such statements would be required, of course.

To summarize, in planning change, the first phase is unfreezing the organization. This means creating awareness of the need for change. This is best done by contrasting an actual with a more desired state. Also critical to this initial planning phase is leadership, in this case, leadership capable of establishing conditions whereby the desired future state can be determined. And, finally, for adequate planning, the political and power dynamics within the organization must be addressed. Addressing these organizational dynamics means involving informal leaders in the planning and making certain that the way the future state is described is responsive to organizational members' inevitable question, "What's in it for me?"

Managing the Change Process

The toughest job is to *manage* the change process. In writing about this management process, I can be logical, rational, and perhaps convey that dealing with organizational change is indeed subject to management. In reality, however, managing change is sloppy—people never do exactly as we plan. And it follows Murphy's Law—if anything can go wrong, it will. Moreover, organizational politics is always present and change, after all, affects us all emotionally.

Even with these qualifications and the perspective that managing change is not always manageable, it is useful to consider certain principles and guidelines. The more a process may seem unmanageable, the more we should stick closely to those activities that have been demonstrated to be helpful. The following principles and guidelines meet the criterion of demonstrated helpfulness.

Disengagement from the Past

Once it has been decided that change will happen and the planning has occurred, or is in process, time and energy need to be devoted to disengaging from the past, that is, from certain ways of working; from a program, project, or product; from a geographical location; or from a group of people with whom one previously worked. Disengagement may take a variety of forms. An event can be held to recognize in a formal way the contribution of a certain program that will no longer be implemented, and of the people who were involved. The event can be celebratory in nature despite conclusion of the program.

In an organization with which I am familiar, a particular program was to be phased out to make way for a new and different one. The program had involved research and development on a rocket used by NASA and the U.S. Air Force that became obsolete. Yet R&D was conducted with the rocket program all along the way as if it would always exist and be constantly improved. After almost twenty years with this program the engineers and technicians involved were to be reassigned or encouraged to retire early. Change came surely and swiftly for these rocket professionals. Before taking on a new program and having to acquire some new knowledge and learn new skills, senior management conducted a brief ceremony. On the front lawn in front of the administration building a table draped in black cloth was the focal point. Underneath the cloth was a small replica of the old rocket. After the table was uncovered, certain senior managers made very brief speeches extolling the former program and the people who had contributed to it over the years. All drank a toast, and the rocket was then covered again, symbolically buried. The head of the organization then gave a short explanation of the new program (solar energy for propulsion in space) that was replacing the old. The entire event took less than thirty minutes. Accomplished with this event were two important outcomes: First, an unequivocal symbolic act demonstrated the end of the program, and, second, affirmative recognition was provided for those who had been involved.

While one may not need to conduct a funeral or demonstrate an ending quite as dramatically, two critical principles of managing change should be considered, both tied directly to human emotion. One is the principle of "unfinished business" and the other concerns appealing to rather than ignoring people's feelings of pride.

Unfinished business.   When something is incomplete we humans tend to attempt some form of completion. A simple example from introductory psychology is when viewing a figure such as the following,

we "psychologically" close the gap and complete mentally what we believe to be a circle. Less simple, but based on the same principle, is the situation when we have an argument with someone that soon stops for one reason or another yet remains unresolved; one tends to continue the argument mentally even though the other party is no longer present. We spend mental and emotional energy in an attempt to finish, to resolve, to complete the argument. So it is with organizational change. When newness is thrust on organizational members replacing, say, former ways of doing things with no time to disengage and "finish the business" of the former way, they will spend energy trying to deal with the incompleteness. This energy may take the form of continuing simply to talk about the former ways, or criticizing the new ways as clearly imperfect, or even more resistantly, sabotaging the new ways. What is referred to as "resistance to change" often reflects energy devoted to closure attempts. Providing some way for organizational members to disengage, to finish, at least to some extent, the past helps them to focus on the change and the future.

I am not the first to relate this important human principle to organizational change. Nadler (1981), building on the theoretical writings of Lewin and the work of Beckhard and Harris (1977), discusses this disengagement process in his integration of a number of managing change principles. He categorizes managing change into three broad needs or challenges: (1) the need to motivate change (including disengagement), (2) the need to manage the transition, where he elaborates on Beckhard and Harris, and (3) the need to shape the political dynamics of change. My treatment of this managing change section reflects Nadler's thinking as well as others', for example, Tichy (1983) and Tichy and Devanna (1986).

Pride. Even though pride is among the seven deadly sins, it can be appealed to in a positive way. People who have worked in a particular job over a period of years typically build feelings of personal pride in what they do. Sometimes when change comes and people are told they must now do things differently, not their old jobs anymore, an implied message may be that what they used to do is now wrong and no longer worthwhile. Often the tendency on the part of management is to want to "get on with it" and quickly forget the past. We no longer need to manufacture that product, provide that service, and so on.

The point is that when change takes place and no time is given to recognize that even though an era had ended, what organizational members had been doing was worthwhile, they will tend to feel less worthwhile themselves. The stronger this feeling, the more organizational members' energy will be focused on dealing with their wounded pride. Usually a simple yet formal recognition that people had worked on important products or services for the organization and that significant contributions were made will be sufficient. This kind of act again helps organizational members to deal with potentially strong human emotions, to achieve some degree of closure, and gradually to disengage from the past.

Communication. It is difficult to communicate too much during a major change effort. It is possible, of course. One can communicate so much that the messages begin to raise people's expectations unduly. Just as important as the quantity of communicating is, of course, the content. Moreover, communicating what will remain the same is as important as communicating what will be different. Wisdom from the world of counseling and clinical psychology is relevant here.

To help individuals cope with and manage change in their lives, the wisdom is that of keeping something stable in one's life while changing other aspects. It is not wise to change one's career, quit one's job, and get a divorce all at the same time. Holding on to something that is *not* changing in one's life—having an anchor, as it were—helps one significantly to deal with the complexity of change in other parts.

The same is true at an organizational level. People can more adequately deal with and manage what may be considerable chaos and complexity with respect to an organizational change effort if they know that some aspects of the organization will remain stable—at least for the time being. We can more easily handle, say, a major overhaul of the organization's structure and even accompanying changes in our jobs if we can at the same time be assured that, for example, our compensation will not change; that is, the organization's reward system will remain intact.

Managing the Transition

As Beckhard and Harris (1987) emphasize, creating a transition management team can be very important and useful to the change process. The larger and more complex the change effort, the more systematic, concentrated attention needs to be paid to the management process. An occasional committee or task force meeting may not do the job. It may be wise to appoint a person to manage the transition full-time with others assigned on a part-time basis. Large, complex change will not manage itself; that's the point. For a later version of this kind of thinking, see Beckhard and Pritchard (1992). Other important factors to manage in the change process, as Nadler (1981) had highlighted, are the following:

Involvement. As noted before, a principle of behavior that is central to effective management, in general, and managing change, in particular, is "Involvement leads to commitment." Stated a bit more elaborately, the degree to which people will be committed to an act is a function of the degree to which they have been involved in determining what that act will be.

For organizational change to occur effectively, it is imperative to involve certain key individuals (opinion leaders), perhaps on a singular, one-on-one basis. But, in general, it is more effective to direct change at the group level than at the individual level.

If one attempts to change an attitude or the behavior of an individual without attempting to change the same behavior or attitude in the group to which the individual belongs, then the individual will be a deviate and either will come under pressure from the group to get back into line or will be rejected entirely. Thus, the major leverage point for change is at the group level; for example, by modifying a group norm or standards. Recall from Chapter 3 a key aspect from Kurt Lewin's theory:

> As long as group standards are unchanged, the individual will resist change more strongly the farther he is to depart from group standards. If the group standard itself is changed, the resistance which is due to the relation between individuals and group standard is eliminated. (Lewin, 1958: 120)

For a much later and well-documented rationale for involving people in organizational life, in general, and particularly, in change efforts, see Lawler (1992).

Continuing with this involvement theme, let us now further consider the importance of including people in the implementation of goals.

For any given change goal, there will likely be multiple paths to that goal. Some of these paths may be more efficient than others, but most if not all paths that people can think of will lead to goal accomplishment. Because of circumstances leaders and managers of change may not always involve organizational members to any significant degree in establishing the primary goals. For purposes of gaining commitment, involving organizational members in the planning of *how to reach* those goals is critical, however.

To repeat, there are usually different ways to reach a singular goal and no one way is always clearly superior. Thus, delegating decisions of implementation, that is, allowing organization members who must carry out the plans for reaching the goal to determine for themselves the plans for getting there will increase overall commitment to the change effort.

To gain their commitment, it is beneficial to involve people in decisions that will directly affect them. At times, however, only a few executives will have the requisite information or relevant experience for optimizing the effectiveness of decisions regarding goals. Under these conditions, executives can carefully explain to organizational members the logic underlying a change decision and they will typically accept the change goal. To proceed with telling them in detail about how to reach the goal is to risk resistance. The point is that executives can more easily win acceptance for a predetermined goal, provided the goal is viewed as challenging yet reasonable, than they can have a predetermined implementation plan accepted. Commitment, therefore, can be gained by involving organizational members in the transition planning.

Multiple Leverage.   Often managers of change rely too heavily on a singular system lever to move the organization toward the desired change. The lever most often chosen is structure. "Changing the organizational chart will do the job" is a frequent assumption. But in a study of successful versus unsuccessful OD efforts, Burke, Clark, and Koopman (1984) found that the intervention most associated with lack of success was a change in the structure and that intervention was the only change made.

In large, complex organizations composed of many subsystems, when one of these subsystems is changed eventually all other subsystems will be affected. This principle is based on sound, general system theory (Katz and Kahn, 1978). Therefore, when managing change multiple systems, or levers, must be considered. At the top of the list is mission and strategy. A change in strategy best precedes structural change (Chandler, 1962). Moreover, when a structural change is made, changes in the management information system are likely to be required. Since it is also likely that different management practices will be needed, changes in the reward system to reinforce these new practices will help to ensure the overall success of the change effort. These points follow from the discussion of the Burke–Litwin model and the British Airways example in the previous chapter.

The general idea to keep in mind, then, is the fact that organizations are dynamic, open systems. Changing an organization successfully requires that attention be paid to its multiplicity of subsystems, or levers, in tandem and in mutual support of the overall effort.

Feedback. In the face of ambiguity about how things are going, people more often than not assume the worst. "I knew this change wouldn't work!" To keep momentum, positive energy directed toward the change goal(s), providing feedback to organizational members about progress, regardless of how minor the progress may be, will help. Periodic progress reports, additional information incorporated within the management information system, conducting brief celebratory events when a change milestone is reached, are examples of how to monitor progress and, more importantly, ways to provide organizational members with relevant feedback.

Symbols and Language. To keep organizational members focused and oriented, it is beneficial to have some symbol, acronym, or slogan to represent the change goal(s). The marketing department can be helpful with this process.

It is not always possible to state change goals in clear simple statements. While a new organizational strategy or mission may be clear in the minds of senior management, since they have perhaps discussed and debated it for months and months, when put in writing, the new strategy may come across to the majority of people in the organization as vague, quite general, and abstract. Using a symbol may help not only to simplify and clarify the change goal but to capture organizational members' imagination and enthusiasm as well. A change in strategy from a technology-driven organization to a customer-driven one might, for example, be symbolized by a question inscribed on, say, a paperweight for each organizational member's desk or work area, which asks "Have you talked with a customer today?"

An actual example, one with which I had some personal involvement, was created for a specific group within the change effort at British Airways (see Chapter 7). The example concerned a training of trainers program for selected line managers. They were trained to help conduct a one-week residential "Managing People First" (MPF) program for upper-middle and midlevel management, well over 1000 managers in total. Although couched within a training of trainers objective, the large, broader objective was to indoctrinate sixteen hand-picked, high-potential managers with the underlying rationale for the specific MPF program and for the overall BA cultural change effort. Their broader mandate called for them to be change agents, to model the new behaviors associated with the desired culture. I referred to them as "culture carriers." They were to help leverage change. Our symbol for them was a lever with a hand gripping it and the accompanying slogan was the Greek philosopher Archimedes' famous quote, to paraphrase in English, "Give me a fulcrum [lever] and a place to stand, and I will move the world."

Stabilizing the Change

Actually a part of the stabilization process should begin during the disengagement stage. Just as important for organizational members to learn about what will be different is to be informed about what will *not* change. During times of significant change, when people are clear about what is not changing amid all that is, they have something stable to hold on to, an anchor. For example, even though an organization might be changing its strategy and structure, people could still be rewarded for their performance as before, say, on merit. If they can count on their rewards being administered as before, this element of stability will help them cope with the uncertainties. As a close friend once said to me years ago, "Never try to change everything at once."

The reward system is central to stabilizing change once it is underway. As new practices begin to occur, as people begin to behave in ways that help to move the organization toward the change goal(s), and as milestones are reached, the reward system should be deployed to reinforce these new, "right" behaviors and directions. As Tom Peters has put it, "Catch people doing the right thing."

Formally and publicly recognizing people for having helped to move the organization in the change direction not only will serve to reinforce and stabilize the new behaviors but will send a clear signal as well to others in the organization as to what the "right" behaviors are.

A final process of stabilizing the change, and clearly not mutually exclusive from the above points regarding the reward system, is to arrange for certain organizational members to serve as "guardians" of the new way of doing things (Hornstein, et al., 1971). They serve primarily as role models, as "norm carriers" of the new culture. Provided these people are carefully selected and strategically placed in the organization, that is, they are seen as powerful leaders and representative of the future, they can help significantly to stabilize the change.

Summary

By way of summary, refer to Table 8.1. The model depicts the three broad phases of planning, managing, and stabilizing the change effort as well as the more specific activities recommended for each phase.

Theory About Culture Change[*]

Consulting work on business strategy or implementing the vision is stronger today than ever. In fact, when speaking to groups about my consulting efforts, I characterize myself as working in the "McKinsey aftermarket." (Substitute the name of any number of other so-called traditional management consulting firms, and my point would remain the same. I simply have followed McKinsey more than any other name brand.) In response to a firm's desire to change its strategy or structure, a team from one of these big-name consulting firms sweeps into the client organization and changes things. Approximately six months later someone like myself is called in to help make these changes work, the big names having left the scene. I ask questions about the organization's culture and typically find that it hasn't been touched. I then initiate a discussion about the possible alignment of the culture with the new strategy, if not new mission; the point being that unless key aspects of the culture are modified to fit the new mission or strategy, the latter will not work. Now to some fundamentals about culture change.

When I begin a discussion with an audience about culture change, I like to start by writing these three words on an easel pad or overhead projection:

- Values
- Attitudes
- Behavior

---

[*]This section is taken in part from Burke (1993).

Table 8.1
A Model for Managing Change

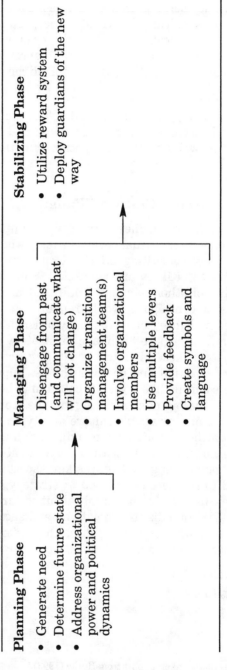

Planning Phase	Managing Phase	Stabilizing Phase
• Generate need	• Disengage from past (and communicate what will not change)	• Utilize reward system
• Determine future state	• Organize transition management team(s)	• Deploy guardians of the new way
• Address organizational power and political dynamics	• Involve organizational members	
	• Use multiple levers	
	• Provide feedback	
	• Create symbols and language	

and then I ask people to rank these terms according to degree of difficulty to change. Practically everyone agrees that the order presented is the proper ranking from most difficult, *values,* to least, *behavior.* Not that behavior change is simple to do, but comparatively speaking, among the three, behavior is the least difficult.

I then make the point that you do not change culture by directly attempting to change culture; that is, values, norms, deeply held beliefs and attitudes, long-standing historical precedence—the primary ingredients of an organization's culture. You begin instead with the least difficult aspect to change: behavior.

Of course, you begin by determining what you want the new culture to be (in the case of British Airways, it was to become more service oriented and customer focused), followed by an identification of the behaviors required to realize that new and different culture. You work on managers first by identifying as specifically as possible the kinds of behavioral practices that will be manifestations of the desired culture; such as, for example, "Communicating with others in an open and frank manner," or "Involving subordinates in decisions that directly affect their work." Next you train managers in these behavioral practices primarily via feedback and role or skill practice. Then you include these new practices in managers' performance appraisals and incorporate pay for performance so that the more managers actually use the practices the more incentive pay they receive. To summarize, first you announce the change regarding the culture. Second, you get managers' attention by training them in the practices. Third, you measure their degree of use of the practices. And, finally, you reward them when they employ the practices. These were steps followed in the British Airways change effort (see Chapter 7).

I have grossly oversimplified the complicated change process. So, let me ground this summary in a theory you may have heard in Psychology 101—the James–Lange theory. In essence, the theory is stated as follows: "I am afraid because I run" is more accurate than "I run because I am afraid."

At first this sounds illogical. Around the turn of this century the two theorists, James and Lange, the former a psychologist and the latter a physiologist, stated essentially the same idea independent of each other—that we act first and then attribute to that act a reason or at least a label for the action.

Many years later, Stan Schacter (1959) conducted a series of laboratory experiments with humans that provided considerable support for the James–Lange theory. I have been a fan of the theory for a long time and follow the reasoning when consulting about planning and managing change in an organization's culture.

We first get managers to move behaviorally in the direction of the desired culture. At British Airways, this was the "Managing People First" program. We provide certain labels for clusters of these behaviors. These labels are actually values. Again, in the case of British Airways, these cluster labels of values (a total of four) were *clarity and helpfulness, promoting achievement, influencing through personal excellence and teamwork,* and *care and trust.* As managers begin to move (behave) in the desired direction, they get rewarded for doing so. As they behave and get rewarded for it every time, they begin to believe that this new way of managing is actually a good thing. If they believe it is good then a value has been affected, and values, in part, comprise culture.

Eventually, then, culture change has begun to occur—but you act first, then help with reasons, labels, and values. All this may and probably should be stated at the outset. "With the new, desired culture we are attempting to adhere to a revitalized mission with a different strategy that will be supported by those values (for example, to be number 1 in customer service)." Organizational members' reactions are likely to be "Sounds good, but we'll see . . ." or "I'll believe it when I see it." So, for the sake of actual change, you plunge ahead with the behaviors because if you delay by trying to explain and explain, the "we'll see" attitude will never be addressed.

Even grounded in some theory, you may still say that it is more complicated than that—and you would be correct. Beginning in the mid-1980s, and particularly with my work at British Airways, I felt a strong need for a larger organizational framework that would help to guide the change effort. This need led to George Litwin and my developing a broader organizational model of performance and change that we found to be very useful for planning and managing change in large, complex systems such as BA (Burke and Litwin, 1992; see Chapter 7). The point is that it is critical to conceptualize culture in a broader framework.

In summary, one does not change (or shape) organizational culture by trying to change organizational culture directly. Values, perhaps the essential ingredient of culture, are difficult to change. First, then, leaders must identify the critical values. Second, rather than announce the values and expect employees to adopt them (not unlike trying to shape or change culture by directly trying to change it), organizational leaders must provide ways for the values to be incorporated within people's behavior. Thus, after providing the direction, the value choice is clearly the first step, the next immediate step is behavioral. Remember that behavior is easier, in relative terms to be sure, to change and shape than values and attitudes.

Measuring Progress of the Change Effort

How can you tell if you are making any progress in a change effort? My general answer to this question is, "Not in the most obvious ways." There are at least four ways to tell.

1. The quantity of problems that organizational members must handle may not decrease. In the short run, it may even increase. A clear sign of progress, though, is that the nature of problems has changed. Organization members are dealing with new and different problems.

2. When organizational members express frustration about lack of progress regarding change, as paradoxical as it may seem such expression is a clear sign of progress. People are complaining about the right things. The following illustration should help to clarify this point.

During the early 1960s Abraham Maslow spent a summer observing work in a high-tech company in Southern California. He kept a diary of his observations and later converted it into a book (Maslow, 1965). One of his observations stands out for me—his distinction between grumbles and meta-grumbles. Grumbles are complaints about relatively small matters: "We never seem to have enough copy machines that are in good operating condition." "Why can't someone arrange for better maintenance of this building?" In other words, the grumbles concern hygiene factors, to use Herzberg's term, those aspects of work life that contribute to one's level of dissatisfaction. Meta-grumbles, on the other hand, are complaints about such things as lack of clarity about goals, people needing to have more autonomy in carrying out their assignments, or expressing a desire for greater teamwork and collaboration. These complaints are about broader organizational concerns, usually beyond an individual matter. Maslow contended that managers should be happy to hear meta-grumbles, that underneath such complaining was motivation to be tapped and directed for the good of the overall organization. So it is in assessing progress toward change. Meta-grumbles should be music to management's ears.

3. When issues, concerns, and progress reports regarding the change effort routinely become a part of the agenda for regular managers and staff meetings, that is a sign of progress. This means that the change effort is being monitored and constantly attended to.

4. And, finally, indicative of progress are special events held from time to time that assess progress, reevaluate the direction, celebrate milestones achieved, and recognize individuals for their accomplishments in helping with the change effort.

Summary

In this chapter we have considered the planning and management of change. The overall process is what OD practitioners refer to as the intervention phase. According to Argyris (1970) an effective intervention is one that (1) provides *valid information* for the client organization, (2) allows for *choice* by the client regarding the specific steps to be taken, and (3) leads to *commitment* on the client's part to those action steps for change.

In planning change it is important, first, to assure that a need for change is determined if not developed and, second, to address the power and political dynamics of the organization. Managing the change effort is essentially transition management and concerns disengaging from the past, communicating with people about the change, involving people in implementation planning, organizing a transition management team, using multiple leverages, providing feedback and creating symbols and language to help focus the effort. The final phase, stabilizing the change, consists of utilizing the reward system to reinforce the new "ways of doing things" and putting into place key individuals to serve as "guardians" of the change goal(s).

Since I have stipulated that OD is a process of change in the organization's culture, it is imperative that we are grounded in theory about this kind of change and that we conceptualize our effort within some overall framework or model.

Four ways to assess progress toward the change were covered. The four—different problems, meta-grumbles, change concerns as a regular part of a meeting agenda, and progress review events—were described as not-so-obvious ways to determine progress.

9

Does OD Work?

"Does it work?" is one of the first questions managers ask about anything new. This chapter therefore responds to the question first by showing that there is substantial evidence that OD does indeed work. Caveats will be considered as we respond further to the question. Next we shall consider obstacles to conducting an evaluation, the seventh phase of any OD effort, and finally we shall conclude by arguing the importance of evaluation regardless of the problems involved and the pressures against such an activity.

Does It Work?

When OD is done according to the principles and practices expounded in this brief volume, my experience is that OD works. But my experience and others' experience in "successfully" practicing OD is not enough. So-called hard evidence is needed. And, indeed, there is evidence. French and Bell (1978), selected nine studies that support OD's effectiveness. Four of their nine, for example, were studies by Beckhard and Lake (1971), Kimberly and Nielsen (1975), King (1974), and Marrow, Bowers, and Seashore (1967).

Other studies could be included in the French and Bell list, such as the one by Golembiewski, Hilles, and Kagno (1974).

There are problems, however. From a survey of sixty-three organizations regarding their knowledge and use of organization development, Heisler (1975) found, among other things, that the major criticism of OD efforts was the difficulty in evaluating their effectiveness. A number of others have made similar observations, see, for example, King, Sherwood, and Manning (1978), Morrison (1978), Porras (1979), and Porras and Patterson (1979).

More recently researchers, in attempting to evaluate the effectiveness of OD, have relied on a method called meta-analysis. The value of meta-analysis is that it is a statistical technique that summarizes and integrates numerous findings across many studies. As Guzzo, Jette, and Katzell (1985) point out,

> Through meta-analysis, a common yardstick for measuring results of different studies is obtained that furnishes a level of integration of studies not possible through traditional judgmental ways of reviewing a body of literature. In fact, proponents of meta-analysis have criticized traditional literature review methods for their susceptibility to bias and insensitivity to artificial sources of differences in results. (p. 276)

In their meta-analysis of eleven types of OD activities Guzzo et al. showed that these "psychologically based organizational interventions," as they referred to them, raised worker productivity. These interventions included job design, participative management, sociotechnical systems, and team building. This finding was based on their analysis of ninety-eight studies.

In their meta-analysis of 126 research studies, Neuman, Edwards, and Raju (1989) found that OD interventions had a stronger and positive effect on worker attitudes and satisfaction on the job. Their analysis further showed that multiple OD interventions, for example, team building, say, plus job enrichment, survey feedback, and so on, had a much stronger effect than singular OD interventions.

So, there is evidence.

There are problems, nevertheless, in attempting to evaluate OD interventions. We shall now consider the nature of some of these problems and issues.

Research Issues in Evaluating OD Efforts

The overriding issue in OD evaluation is purpose—whether the research effort is evaluation or knowledge generation, whether it is for the benefit of the client or the social scientist. Since we are discussing evaluation, that should be the obvious concern, not scientific generation of knowledge; but the assessment methodology—how we collect and analyze our information for evaluative purposes—is based on the traditional scientific method. We control and manipulate some independent variables, make some interventions, and see if any difference occurs with respect to some dependent variables. We decide to use team building as an intervention, for example, and we collect information (a dependent variable) to see if it made any difference. We might use a questionnaire to ask team members if they feel more satisfied with and committed to the team, and we might determine if the team's work performance increases after the team building effort has occurred. Even if our data showed increased satisfaction, commitment, and work performance, it would be difficult to demonstrate that the team building intervention has *caused* these outcomes unless we had also collected data from a matched control group, a similar team for which no team building had been done, and could compare data for the same period for the two groups. Another critical factor in this evaluation would be the people who collect and analyze the data. Numerous studies have shown that the researcher can affect the outcome (Rosenthal, 1976). This brings up the question of objectivity. To be scientific, or objective, the researcher should be someone other than the team building consultant or the organization members involved.

Argyris (1968) has argued, however, that the more scientific the evaluation is, the less it is likely to be relevant to and therefore used by the client. Schein (1992) in his study of organizational culture has made similar arguments.

To be more specific, we shall now examine some primary research issues and problems associated with the evaluation of an organization development effort. The issues and problems are addressed in the form of six questions, which are not necessarily mutually exclusive.

What Is Organizational Effectiveness?   In general, the goal of an OD effort is to improve the organization, to make it more effective, whether the effort is with a large, total system or with a division—a subsystem of a larger organization. It is not a simple matter to define effectiveness (Goodman and Pennings, 1980) or to get people to agree on a definition.

Cameron (1980) points out that there are at least four different criteria for organizational effectiveness and that these criteria differ significantly from one organization to another. The differences are particularly apparent when comparing profit-making with nonprofit organizations. The four criteria or models are as follows:

> *The goal model.* Organizational effectiveness is defined in terms of the extent to which the organization accomplishes its goals.
>
> *The system resource model.* Effectiveness is equated with the ability to acquire needed resources.
>
> *The process model.* Effectiveness is defined in terms of how smoothly the organization functions, especially the degree of absence of internal strain in the organization.
>
> *The strategic constituencies model.* Effectiveness is determined by the extent to which the organization satisfies all its strategic constituencies—special interest groups.

As Cameron notes, these models or definitions of effectiveness may be useful or inappropriate, depending on the type of organization and the public or market it tries to serve.

It should thus be apparent that determining organizational effectiveness is not simple.

What Is OD? As illustrated in this book, OD is many things, and there are seven major phases in an OD effort. For evaluative research purposes, do we consider all these phases or just the intervention phase? Moreover, different OD interventions will also result in different outcomes (Neuman, Edwards, and Raju, 1989; Porras, 1979). The more specific and precise we can be in defining the variety of activities coming under the rubric of OD, the more we will be in a position to evaluate the effectiveness of these activities. A way of increasing this precision is to achieve greater clarity about the remaining four questions.

What Is the Independent Variable? In an examination of thirty-eight research studies conducted on various aspects of OD, Pate, Nielsen, and Bacon (1977) reported that they had considerable difficulty in categorizing variables from the studies. They could not be sure whether the independent variable was the OD intervention itself or whether OD was only instrumental in the manipulation of some other independent variable. They took the view that OD is instrumental but does not constitute the independent variable as such. "For example, one might expect introduction of participative decision making (OD intervention) to facilitate worker awareness of the rationale for organizational actions (independent variable), which in turn may increase support and commitment to those actions (dependent variables)" (pp. 450–51). Their emphasis of this issue is helpful because we can now be clearer about what activities to evaluate specifically.

How Can We Control Variables? As organizations are dynamic systems, this is a question of causal attribution—determining whether the consequences of a change can be attributed to organization development. As noted earlier, the more we can control our research conditions (for example, by having a control condition or control group for comparison) the more we will be able to state with confidence what is cause and what is effect. In dynamic, changing organizations, however, this is almost impossible to do. It is difficult, for example, to persuade a manager to subject his or her organization to a series of time-consuming data-collection activities for the purpose of providing a control group. The manager is likely to ask, "What's in it for us?" It is even more difficult to find an appropriate control group. There are rarely two subsystems within an organization, much less two distinct organizations, that do the same things, have the same types of people, and are managed the same way.

With so much going on in the organizational world and with most of this array of activities being impossible to control, we have what Campbell and Stanley (1966) refer to as a problem of internal validity: determining whether what we did by way of change made a measurable difference. In the absence of pure control group conditions, the true experimental design for research purposes, Campbell and Stanley have provided what they call quasi-experimental designs. These designs, though not perfect from a research perspective, provide ways for controlling certain conditions so that validity will be enhanced. Their time-series design is a good example. In this design several measures are taken at certain intervals *before* the intervention and several measures are taken at essentially the same intervals *after* the intervention.

If it can be shown (1) that there are no significant differences among the first, say, four observations, (2) that there are significant changes from the first four to the fifth observation and beyond (that is, after the intervention), and (3) that there are then no significant differences among, say, four observations after the intervention, then the differences that occurred between preintervention and postintervention must be a result of the change, not merely the passage of time or other variables.

What Changed? Golembiewski, Billingsley, and Yeager (1976) drew distinctions among three types of change, which they labeled alpha, beta, and gamma. *Alpha* change concerns a difference that occurs along some relatively stable dimension of reality. This change is typically a comparative measure before and after an intervention. If comparative measures of trust among team members showed an increase after a team-building intervention, for example, then we might conclude that our OD intervention had made a difference. Golembiewski et al. assert that most OD evaluation research designs consist of such before-and-after self-reports.

Suppose, however, that a decrease in trust occurred—or no change at all. One study has shown that, although no decrease in trust occurred, neither did a measurable increase occur as a consequence of team-building intervention (Friedlander, 1970). Change may have occurred, however. The difference may be what Golembiewski, Billingsley, and Yeager call a *beta* change, a recalibration of the intervals along some constant dimension of reality. As a result of team-building intervention, team members may view trust very differently. Their basis for judging the nature of trust changed, rather than their perception of a simple increase or decrease in trust along some stable continuum.

A *gamma* change "involves a redefinition or reconceptualization of some domain, a major change in the perspective or frame of reference within which phenomena are perceived and classified, in what is taken to be relevant in some slice of reality" (Golembiewski, Billingsley, and Yeager, 1976: 135). This involves change from one state to another. Staying with the example, after the intervention team members might conclude that trust was not a relevant variable in their team building experience. They might believe that the gain in their clarity about roles and responsibilities was the relevant factor and that their improvement as a team had nothing to do with trust.

Thus, selecting the appropriate dependent variables—determining specifically what might change—is not as simple as it might appear. This is especially important when self-report data are used.

Who Will Conduct the Research and Who Will Use the Results?   The last issue to be addressed is the people involved in the evaluation effort. To avoid the possibility of a Pygmalion effect and to increase the probability of objectivity, it is best that the researcher be someone other than the OD consultant. Both the researcher and the consultant are interveners into the organization, however, and therefore it is imperative that they collaborate. The researcher needs to know not only the consultant's overall strategy—change goals, targets, and so forth—and what interventions might be used, but also the consultant's predictions concerning what should change as a result of the OD effort.

The people who will make decisions as a result of the evaluation research must be involved. These people may or may not be directly involved in the OD process itself, but the decision makers need to be involved by the researcher in much the same way that the organization members who are directly involved in the OD process would be participating in the research goals, methods, and interpretation. This involvement of the decision makers helps ensure that the research results will be valid and will be utilized for further decision making.

In addition to these issues and inherent problems in evaluating OD efforts there are a number of pressures against conducting this seventh phase of an OD effort. We shall now examine some of these more important obstacles.

Pressures Opposed to Evaluation

The evaluation process of OD practice can be compared to an annual physical examination: Everyone agrees that it should be done, but no one, except a highly motivated researcher, wants to go to the trouble and expense of making it happen. We shall examine first some of the reasons for opposing evaluation and then conclude with reasons for going ahead with this phase.

There are at least four sets of people involved in or related to OD evaluation: the manager or decision maker, the organization members who are directly involved in the OD process (the manager or decision maker may or may not be in this process), the OD consultant, and the evaluation researcher. There are pressures on each of these categories of people to ignore evaluation.

The Manager or Decision Maker. Managers want results. If interventions in an OD effort are accompanied by change in certain organizational areas that are important to managers, such as increased profits, decreased absenteeism, or increased morale, that is often all that is necessary for a manager to choose to continue with OD or to move on to other things. Managers want to know *if* it works, not *why* it works. Such managers are usually found in fast-moving, marketing-oriented organizations, where short-term results are rewarded. There are other types of managers, however.

Managers in highly technical, scientific organizations may take the opposite stance. These managers might argue that, unless you can measure the consequences of an organization development effort in a rigorous, scientific manner, an evaluation is not worth doing.

Opposition to evaluation research from managers who are in key decision-making roles may take either extreme: evaluation research is not necessary because the outcomes are self-evident or because the effects of OD cannot be measured scientifically. Other reasons for opposition from managers could be the cost involved, the amount of extra time it will take, or the undesirability of an outsider coming in to do research on them.

The Organization Members Involved in the OD Effort. Opposition from those directly involved in the OD process may take the same forms as those mentioned with respect to the managers or decision makers. In addition to those possible if not highly potential forms of opposition, organization members may complain about the time it will take for them to answer the questionnaires, for example, when this time could be utilized more productively in getting on with further aspects of the OD effort. They also might argue that the research staff is likely to be more beneficial to the goals of the researcher than to the goals of the organization's change effort.

The OD Consultant. The OD consultant is likely to want an evaluation study but for reasons that differ from those of the manager or decision maker. Managers are interested in OD's impact on outcomes—profits, turnover, costs, productivity—OD consultants may be more interested in process—the impact that OD may have on behavior, attitudes, organizational procedures, changes in authority relationships, and the like. A study by Porras and Wilkens (1980) indicates that many OD consultants may be disappointed with evaluation research on organization development. Porras and Wilkens found that OD in a large organization had a positive impact on outcomes, such as unit performance, but a negative consequence for attitudinal and behavioral variables that described organizational and individual processes. As Porras and Wilkens noted, these latter, unexpected negative findings may reflect a beta change, not an alpha change (Golembiewski, Billingsley, and Yeager, 1976), since their measures of attitudes and behavior were through self-report questionnaires whereas their measures of unit performance came from company records.

The point here is not that OD consultants are uninterested in or opposed to determining OD's impact on outcomes but that certain factors may be more important to the consultant as a professional.

The Evaluation Researcher. The researcher is interested in both outcome and process measures, but his or her objectives for the use of the research results may differ from those of the other three groups of people concerned with an OD effort. The researcher is often more interested in contributing to the body of knowledge concerning organizations as changing systems or the effectiveness of organization development as a field than in providing information for the organization's decision makers. This difference in objectives or priorities can cause problems with planning and implementing an evaluation research effort, but opposition on the part of a researcher toward conducting an evaluation study is likely to occur for another reason. Most researchers are trained only according to the traditional scientific method of research, which involves distancing oneself from and controlling the subjects of the research (client), not collaborating with them.

Reasons for Conducting the Evaluation Phase

The forces that oppose evaluative research of an organization development effort are formidable and should not be dismissed lightly, but there are also compelling reasons for conducting evaluative research.

Briefly, the primary arguments for an evaluative research study of an OD effort are as follows:

1. An evaluation forces the definition of the change objectives.

2. An evaluation forces the clarification of the change outcomes that are expected.

3. An evaluation forces the clarification of how these change outcomes are to be measured.

4. An evaluation forces specificity with respect to how certain procedures, events, and activities will be implemented.

5. An evaluation helps to signal many of the problems and obstacles to be anticipated in the OD effort.

6. An evaluation facilitates planning for next steps and stages of organizational improvement and development.

As we know from system theory, particularly as applied to organizations, there may be no such thing as a single cause for a single effect. Systematic evaluation will provide many of the casual answers for what occurs and has occurred in organizations. Generally, but perhaps most importantly, evaluation forces clarity about what *effectiveness* is for an organization.

Finally, it is important to conduct some kind of evaluation rather than none at all. And rather than become embroiled in the issues of whether an outside researcher or the OD practitioner conduct the evaluation—and in the spirit of OD practice anyway—perhaps the OD practitioner can *facilitate* an evaluative process; help the client do the job themselves.

Summary

There is sufficiently strong empirical evidence that OD works. The more recent meta-analysis method of research has contributed significantly to our understanding of whether OD works. Yet, as has been pointed out, there are problems and issues in conducting evaluations of OD efforts. It is important, nevertheless, to conduct some kind of evaluation rather than none at all. The paper by Goodstein and Burke (1991) regarding British Airways is an example of an evaluation that is nonscientific and post hoc but data based in part. The data are primarily financial, as is the quantitative information reported by Leahey and Kotter (1990) in their case study of British Airways. In these analyses of BA an assumption is made that OD had an effect in that financial performance significantly improved—but it is assumed, not proven. We can learn from such reports in any case. Moreover, as Argyris, Putnam, and Smith (1985) have indicated, effective OD may actually be inconsistent with rigorous research.

In addition to the contribution of meta-analysis it may also be that more effective work in the practice of OD has made a positive difference, that is, that OD works. Sashkin and Burke (1987) summarize this point as follows:

> We suggest that the clear research demonstration of positive OD impacts owes much to the integration of task structure and behavioral process-based OD approaches and of people-centered with profit-centered OD values. The work on types of change shows an increasingly sophisticated appreciation of the true interdependence of structure and process in OD. (p. 405)

10

The OD Consultant

To be seen as a consultant is to have status, and thus many people aspire to the label and the role. A consultant is one who provides help, counsel, advice, and support, which implies that such a person is wiser than most people.

Although the label *consultant* usually conveys an image of one who provides help, there are obviously many different types of consultants. The purposes of this chapter are to provide a context for the unique role and function of an OD consultant, to consider the different roles and functions of an OD consultant, to explore the kinds of personal characteristics that are needed for OD consultation and the types of people who are in the field, and to suggest ways for those who want to become OD consultants to do so.

Context for Roles and Functions

Where OD Consultants Are Located

Organization development consultants are found either inside an organization, as full-time or part-time employees, or outside organizations, with those organizations considered as clients. Internal consultants are usually located within the human resources, personnel, or employee relations function; they may be part of an OD department and serve exclusively in an OD capacity; or they may combine OD consultation with other duties, such as training, counseling, research, or career assessment and development. Thus, internal OD consultants are usually in a staff function, and they serve line managers throughout the organization.

External OD consultants may be employed by a consulting firm, may be self-employed, or may have academic appointments and consult only part of the time. In the past, external OD consultants usually came from colleges and universities. Now they are more likely to come from consulting firms or work on their own as full-time independent consultants.

Comparisons of the OD Consultant With Other Types of Consultants

Edgar Schein (1987) contrasts the process consultant role, a primary but not exclusive role and function of an OD consultant, with the purchase model and the doctor-patient model. According to Schein, the purchase model is the most prevalent form of consultation, essentially consisting of the client's purchase of expert services information. A client's employment of a consultant to conduct a market research study is an example of purchasing both expert service and information. The doctor-patient model consists of the client's telling the consultant the symptoms of what is wrong with the organization ("Our turnover is too high," "We're losing market share with respect to product X," "Our management information system is a mess") and then expecting the consultant to prescribe a remedy for the problem.

Schein contrasts these two models with the process consultant, one who helps the client organization diagnose its own strengths and weaknesses more effectively, learn how to see organizational problems more clearly, and with the consultant generate a remedy. Schein states:

> It is a key assumption of change that the client must share in the process of diagnosing what may be wrong (or learn to see the problem for himself), and must be actively involved in the process of generating a remedy because only the client ultimately knows what is possible and what will work in his culture and situation. (1987: 30)

Thus the primary though not exclusive function of OD consultants is to help clients learn how to help themselves more effectively. Although consultants occasionally provide expert information and may sometimes prescribe a remedy, their more typical mode of operating is *facilitation*.

While a typical mode, facilitation is not the only function or role of OD consultants. The next section summarizes the array of consultant roles from which OD consultants may choose.

Roles and Functions

Using a continuum from directive to nondirective, Lippitt and Lippitt (1975) have devised a descriptive model of eight different roles for a consultant. By *directive,* Lippitt and Lippitt mean that the consultant's behavior assumes a leadership posture and that he or she initiates activities, whereas at the opposite extreme—nondirective—the consultant merely provides data for the client to use or not. All along the continuum the consultant is active; what varies is how directive or nondirective this activity becomes. The eight roles from directive to nondirective are *advocate, technical specialist, trainer* or *educator, collaborator* (in problem solving), *alternative identifier, fact finder, process specialist,* and *reflector.* Lippitt and Lippitt also note that these roles are not mutually exclusive. The consultant may, for example, serve as a trainer and educator and as an advocate at the same time.

Marginality

As noted earlier in Chapter 5, Margulies (1978) has described the consultant's role differently and more generically. He argues that the OD consultant role is a marginal one. *Marginal* implies being on the periphery, and, accordingly, another term that Margulies uses is *boundary.*

First, Margulies contrasts two models of consulting with which we are already familiar: the *technical* consulting model and the *process* consulting model. His technical consulting model is like Schein's purchase and doctor-patient models and like Lippitt and Lippitt's technical specialist role, and his process model is the same as Schein's process consultation model. Margulies makes an analogy of technical-process with rational-intuitive and with the idea of the two-sided person represented by the two hemispheres of the brain. The OD consultant's role, he argues, is to function between these two halves, in the margin, being neither too technically oriented nor too process-oriented. Both sets of consultant expertise are appropriate, but for the OD consultant neither should be emphasized to the exclusion of the other. The consultant operates within the boundary of these two models of consultation, totally endorsing neither yet accepting both.

Margulies includes two other boundaries: the activities boundary and the membership boundary. For both, the OD consultant should operate at the boundary, in a marginal capacity. With respect to change activities, particularly implementation, the consultant must help but not be directly involved. Suppose, for example, an off-site team-building session for a manager and his subordinates was forthcoming. The consultant would help the manager with the design and process of the meeting but would not lead the meeting.

With respect to membership, the OD consultant is never quite in nor quite out. Although the consultant must be involved, he or she cannot be a member of the client organization. Being a member means that there is vested interest, a relative lack of objectivity. Being totally removed, however, means that the consultant cannot sense, cannot be empathetic, and cannot use his or her own feelings as data for understanding the client organization more thoroughly. Being marginal with respect to membership means that the consultant becomes involved enough to understand client members' feelings and perceptions yet distant enough to be able to see these feelings and perceptions for what they are—someone else's—rather than as an extension of oneself.

Being marginal is critical for both an external consultant and an internal consultant. The major concern regarding the internal OD consultant's role is that he or she can never be a consultant to his or her own group. If the group is an OD department, a member of this department, no matter how skilled, cannot be an effective consultant to it. It is also difficult for an internal OD practitioner to be a consultant to any group that is within the same vertical path or chain of the managerial hierarchy as he or she may be. Since the OD function is often a part of corporate personnel or the human resource function, it would be difficult for the internal OD consultant to play a marginal role in consulting with any of the groups within this corporate function, because the consultant would be a primary organization member of that function. Consulting with marketing, R&D, or manufacturing within one's organization, for example, would be far more feasible and appropriate, since the OD consultant could more easily maintain a marginal role.

It is understandable that an OD consultant's role can be a lonely one. The role can also create anxiety about one's accuracy of perception (no one to check it with but the client) and about one's choice of intervention (whether it is the right thing for the moment). Joining in fully, being a member, helps alleviate this loneliness and anxiety. Staying removed, distant, and aloof can also relieve the anxiety, since feelings are not involved. Doing either, however, lessens one's effectiveness as a consultant significantly. An obvious way to alleviate the problems of loneliness and anxiety is to co-consult. Working as an external and internal consultant team is probably the best way.

Consultants' Abilities

I believe that ten primary abilities are key to an OD consultant's effectiveness. Most of these abilities can be learned, but because of individual differences in personality or basic temperament, some of them would be easier for some people to learn than for others. The effective consultant should have the following abilities:

- The ability to tolerate *ambiguity*. Every organization is different, and what worked before may not work now; every OD effort starts from scratch, and it is best to enter with few preconceived notions other than with the general characteristics that we know about social systems.

- The ability to *influence*. Unless the OD consultant enjoys power and has some talent for persuasion, he or she is likely to succeed in only minor ways in OD. We will consider this point in more detail later.

- The ability to *confront difficult issues*. Much of OD work consists of exposing issues that organization members are reluctant to face.

- The ability to *support and nurture others*. This ability is particularly important in times of conflict and stress; it is also critical just before and during a manager's first experience with team building.

- The ability to *listen well* and *empathize*. This is especially important during interviews, in conflict situations, and when client stress is high.

- The ability to *recognize one's own feelings and intuitions quickly*. It is important to be able to distinguish one's own perceptions from those of the client and also be able to use these feelings and intuitions as interventions when appropriate and timely.

- The ability to *conceptualize*. It is necessary to think and express in understandable words certain relationships, such as the cause-and-effect and if-then linkages that exist within the systemic context of the client organization.

- The ability to *discover* and *mobilize human energy*, both within oneself and within the client organization. There is energy in resistance, for example, and the consultant's interventions are likely to be most effective when they tap existing energy within the organization and provide direction for the productive use of the energy.

- The ability to *teach* or to create learning opportunities. This ability should not be reserved for classroom activities but should be utilized on the job, during meetings, and within the mainstream of the overall change effort.

- The ability to *maintain a sense of humor,* both on the client's behalf and to help sustain perspective: Humor can be useful for reducing tension. It is also useful for the consultant to be able to laugh at himself or herself; not taking oneself too seriously is critical for maintaining perspective about an OD effort, especially since nothing ever goes exactly according to plan, even though OD is supposed to be a *planned* change effort.

In addition to these abilities, it is important, of course, for the OD consultant to have self-confidence and to be interpersonally competent (Argyris, 1970). Finally, I think it is helpful for the consultant to have a sense of mission about his or her work as an OD practitioner. I do not mean to imply that OD consultants should be zealots, but rather that they should believe that what they are doing is worthwhile and potentially helpful to others. This belief helps to sustain energy, to lessen feelings of loneliness and anxiety, and to provide a reason for continuing to work on organizations that appear recalcitrant and impossible to change.

OD Values

Following the line of thought and belief that OD constitutes cultural change, it is obviously important that we understand the nature of organizational values as thoroughly as possible. We also need to understand the value system of the field of OD itself and the carriers of this professional culture—OD practitioners and consultants. Thus, in this section we shall examine the values represented by the field of organization development.

We can gain some understanding of the values represented by OD by referring to the field's roots, especially sensitivity training (see Chapter 3). This method of education and change has a humanistic value orientation, the belief that it is worthwhile for people to have the opportunity throughout their lives to learn and develop personally toward a full realization and actualization of individual potentials. Some people now believe that this preference not only is worthwhile but should be a right or entitlement.

Another OD value that came even more directly from sensitivity training is that people's feelings are just as important a source of data for diagnosis and have as much implication for change as do facts or so-called hard data and people's thoughts and opinions, and that these feelings should be considered as legitimate for expression in the organization as any thought, fact, or opinion.

Yet another OD value stemming from sensitivity training is that conflict, whether interpersonal or intergroup, should be brought to the surface and dealt with directly, rather than ignored, avoided, or manipulated.

Before I go further (my list could continue), let us return to one of the original sources. When sensitivity training was at the height of its popularity in the United States, Schein and

Bennis (1965) stated what they considered its two main value systems: a spirit of inquiry and democracy.

The spirit of inquiry comes from the values of science. Two parts of it are relevant: the hypothetical spirit—being tentative checking on the validity of assumptions, and allowing for error; and experimentalism—putting ideas or assumptions to the test. In sensitivity training, "all experienced behavior is subject to questioning and examination, limited only by the threshold of tolerance to truth and new ideas" (Schein and Bennis, 1965: 32). A corollary value mentioned by Schein and Bennis is being authentic in interpersonal relations.

The second main value system, the democratic value, has two elements: collaboration and conflict resolution through rational means. The learning process in sensitivity training is collaborative between participant and trainer, not a traditional authoritarian student-teacher relationship. By conflict resolution through rational means, Schein and Bennis did not mean that irrational behavior or emotion was off limits, but "that there is a problem-solving orientation to conflict rather than the more traditional approaches based on bargains, power plays, suppression, or compromise" (p. 34).

Most important—what Schein and Bennis called the "overarching and fundamental value" (p. 35)—is the matter of choice. Freedom from coercion and from the arbitrary exercise of authority is the most preferred end state of existence.

Schein and Bennis wrote about and espoused those values in the 1960s, when individualism, rebellion toward authority, and questioning the rights of certain traditional institutions were in vogue. What about OD today? Does the field still maintain the values that evolved from sensitivity training? For some indications let us examine two sources of information: some informal data I have collected and Tichy's (1974) findings.

Next we will cover briefly a study of OD values conducted in the 1990s.

For a number of years I have served as a faculty member in the Columbia Teachers College program, Advanced Organization Development and Human Resource Management. The program is designed for experienced practitioners. One of the sessions I have conducted in this program deals with values. The session involves an exercise in the identification of one's values, primarily those that relate to OD. Since it is difficult to respond to a direct question of what one's values are, and since most of us would tend to respond in a socially desirable manner anyway, I begin the exercise with three other questions:

1. When you are about to contract with a client for possible OD work (an entry situation), what has caused you not to want to be involved, to pull away, not to do it?

2. Give an example of a situation in which you were already involved in an OD effort and then wanted to get out of it.

3. Under what conditions or in what kinds of situations have you felt good or satisfied as a consultant?

After the participants have had time to write their individual responses, I ask them to examine what they have written and to extract or determine from their responses, the values they reveal. I then ask them to state these values in writing, following these guidelines: The statement is a belief I hold, not a "should" for others; the statement communicates right or wrong, good or bad; and the statement cannot be proved quantitatively or scientifically.

In the words of the participants in several of these sessions, involving approximately seventy-five people, mostly male, the following values predominate:

Everyone has the right to learn, grow, and value himself or herself.

It is essential that I, as an OD consultant, respect the right of people to be themselves.

It is right to be insecure about what is right.

I value improving the quality of life.

It is good to move in life toward an ideal self—that is, a congruent self.

An OD consultant's behavior must be congruent with his or her own values.

Value-free OD is a myth and therefore the consultant must clarify and declare his or her assumptions, beliefs, and biases as part of the client's data base for making choices.

OD consultants should help to create environments in which people have the opportunity to *make choices,* to realize their potential, and to contribute to the organization's well being.

We must have a concern for human dignity.

My knowledge and discoveries are "mine"; I can only help others to discover their own.

There have been many more statements, and not all participants agreed with all ten of these statements, but most did. They represent at least part of the OD system of values for these practitioners.

From these statements we can easily draw two conclusions. First, they are well within the mainstream of the earlier values from sensitivity training, even though most of these participants had not been heavily involved in that technique (few would classify themselves as T-group trainers). And second, statements concerning organizations are noticeably absent. It is possible, of course, that this absence results from the nature of my three original questions, but the participants met in small groups after the individual work, and there was an opportunity to broaden their statements.

Also with a small group of OD practitioners, Tichy (1978) found that, although they were concerned with such organizational matters as productivity, they apparently felt somewhat impotent (to use Tichy's term) in bringing about change in these areas. Many admitted, also, that they intervened in areas or with techniques that were not directed at the primary needs or "hurts" of the organization, that they used techniques in which they were skillful and comfortable but that these interventions ultimately did not have much organizational influence.

To repeat a warning, my data and those of Tichy are based on small, select groups of OD practitioners, which may or may not represent the mainstream of consultants in OD work. Thus, we cannot generalize. My personal impression, however, is that these responses are certainly not far off the mark, but may vary in degree. The conclusion, albeit more impressionistic than rigorously scientific, is that most OD practitioners hold these kinds of humanistic values and act accordingly as consultants, believing that organizations should serve humans, not the reverse. Thus, OD consultants more frequently are attracted to and use interventions that help individuals (1) to be more involved in decisions that directly affect them, (2) to be assertive regarding their needs, if not their rights, (3) to plan their careers, (4) to become more a part of the work group, (5) to obtain more interesting jobs or to enrich the ones they have, (6) to have opportunities for additional training, education, and personal development, (7) to be more involved with their superiors in establishing the objectives and quotas they are expected to reach, and, in general, (8) to receive respect and fair treatment.

These values and their consequent interventions in OD are not inappropriate or unneeded. It is painfully obvious that most organizations treat their most valued resources—employees—as if they were expendable. The all-too-frequent attitude among managers is, "If our employees don't like the jobs we provide, they can find employment elsewhere; we pay them a fair wage and they receive excellent fringe benefits." In the name of efficiency and economic or top management pressure, some people in organizations may be bored, some may be discriminated against, and many may be treated unfairly or inequitably regarding their talent and performance. If OD helps correct these imbalances, it is long overdue, but what about the organization? If it doesn't survive, there will be no jobs, no imbalances to correct. Of the two words represented by OD, practitioners heretofore have spent more time on development than on organization. They are equally important, however; if either is out of balance, the OD consultant's goal is to redress the imbalance. Weisbord (1977) has stated it well:

> OD's right goal—its central purpose—grows from its proper setting. If the proper setting is organizations, then there is only one right goal for OD: to confront an issue which most certainly predates the Industrial Revolution. That is the tension between *freedom* and *constraint*. OD's right purpose is to redress *the balance* between freedom and constraint. (p. 4)

He goes on to point out that there is always tension between the two—the autonomy of the individual and the requirements of the organization—and that either can be out of kilter. Furthermore, it is practically impossible to determine the proper balance but, when either factor is obviously out of balance, the OD consultant's goal is to work toward reducing the heavier side.

Related to freedom versus constraint is the potential conflict of individual and organization development versus the so-called bottom line—the demands placed on organizational members, particularly managers and executives, of course, to meet budget or profit goals. With so much pressure in this day and age to meet bottom-line goals, it would not be surprising if the OD values that have been delineated above had taken a back seat. To test this question my colleagues and I (Church and Burke, 1993; Church, Burke and Van Eynde, 1994) conducted a survey of practicing OD consultants. The part of our survey that concerned values revealed that there are three very stable constructs or overarching themes among the thirty-one items in the questionnaire that underlie practitioners' views about the field of OD. These three constructs comprise issues relating to humanistic concerns, business effectiveness, and the external environment. Although the majority of the thirty-one items, when factor analyzed, loaded onto the humanistic dimension, it was the business effectiveness factor that received the highest rating by respondents both in terms of the relative importance of the items for today and in the ideal, even though several of the specific humanistic related *items*—such as empowering employees to act and creating openness in communication—received the highest mean ratings and rankings.

Overall, these findings are quite revealing about the nature and values of OD practitioners in the field today. Although OD people apparently are becoming focused more on emphasizing business and performance issues than on crusading for the humanistic values of the founders, the traditional values have not been entirely lost or abandoned (and appear to be particularly strong in the hearts and minds of practitioners in an ideal sense). These humanistic and process-oriented concerns remain in the duality of shared focus with organizational outcomes that have served to differentiate OD from the beginning, and continue to be an important dichotomy in the practice of the field today. While we had anticipated the existence of this pattern, it was somewhat surprising to note the high degree of consistency between many of the respective value ratings and their associated factor outcomes. It really does suggest that there are only two fundamental dimensions (humanistic and business demands) on which practitioners' perceptions of the values of OD rest (Church and Burke, 1993).

For aspiring OD practitioners, then, it is highly important to understand the values that underlie OD, be able to subscribe to these values, yet be able to live with what may seem to be a contradiction between OD values and business needs. Perhaps a new emerging value of OD is a belief that if one pays attention to human needs and to effective process—that is, *how* business is conducted, especially between people—the so-called bottom line will not only take care of itself but actually improve as a consequence of this kind of attentiveness. The way total quality management, for example, has been described by some (for example, Sashkin and Kiser, 1993; Schuler and Harris, 1992) would clearly support this point of view.

In addition to the compatibility of the quality movement and OD, the greater emphasis now and in the future on diversity and the unambiguous global trends in the corporate world are also fruitful grounds for OD practitioners to cultivate. Examples of useful sources in these areas are Jamieson and O'Mara (1991) regarding diversity and Rhinesmith (1992) and Pucik, Tichy, and Barnett (1992) for the global movement.

Becoming an OD Consultant

I have been asked occasionally how one becomes an OD consultant. I have typically responded with such vague answers as "Well, it depends," since the question is difficult. There simply is no clear and systematic career path for becoming an OD consultant. Experienced people in the field may suggest such paths as going to a training laboratory, taking some psychology courses, tagging along with an experienced consultant to learn by observing and gradually trying some consulting interventions, reading some books, or attending the National Training Laboratories Program for Specialists in Organization Development.

Like any other field that consists of applying skills and implementing a particular kind of practice, experience is the best teacher for OD practice—or rather, experience accompanied by related feedback is the best teacher. One can have numerous experiences, but unless one receives feedback about which experiences are more related to effective practice, then learning rarely occurs. Thus, one should try to obtain experience in and feedback on consultative activities.

The second-best way to become an OD consultant is by some combination of academic learning and nonacademic training.

Academic Training. A number of universities offer a curriculum either in organization development or in related courses. I suggest the following thirteen courses, mostly at the graduate level, that will provide a good background for OD practice. These courses are fairly common, perhaps not all in a single university, but similar courses may be available. Obtaining education in these thirteen subjects would be most useful:

1. *Organizational psychology or organizational behavior.* The former is typically offered in a department of psychology, the latter in a school of business or management. Either course provides the necessary background for understanding human behavior in an organizational context.

2. *Group dynamics.* This kind of course is a must. Organizations are composed of subsystems, usually in the form of work groups or managerial teams. Understanding the theory, research, and conceptual aspects of group behavior as well as the applicability of this knowledge helps one understand the utility of groups in organizations.

3. *Research methods.* Field research methods are preferable since they are the most applicable for learning about data collection and analysis in organizations.

4. *Adult learning.* This type of course is useful for understanding how organization members may learn from their experiences on the job as well as for knowing more about the appropriate rationale for designing training programs.

5. *Career development.* Since OD consultants are frequently involved in designing career development programs and are involved in human resource planning, background in this subject area is important.

6. *Counseling and interviewing.* This kind of course can provide critical skills, not only for diagnosis in general but also for specific help to individual organization members.

7. *Organization development.* Many universities now offer a one-semester or even a two-semester course in OD. The course may not be called OD, so one may have to read course descriptions carefully to find the right one, such as "organization change," "action research," "managing change," etc.

8. *Training and development.* This type of course provides useful information about design of programs and about how to conduct certain learning activities.

9. *Action research and consultation.* This course may be the OD course. It usually offers good experience in data collection for diagnosis, feedback, and planned change. If the specific skills associated with this aspect of consultation are also included, so much the better.

10. *Human resource management.* This course, usually offered in a school of management or business, provides the necessary grounding in the organizational function that is most related to OD.

11. *Process consultation.* A course with this title is not likely to be available, but any course that provides an understanding of what process is and experience in dealing with it, the consultant aspects, should help. Sometimes this topic is covered in a group dynamics course and/or in an OD course. To clarify:

> The process consultant seeks to give the client insight into what is going on around him, within him, and between him and other people. Based on such insight, the consultant then helps the client to figure out what he should do about the situation. But the core of this model is that the client must be helped to remain "pro-active," in the sense of retaining both the diagnostic and remedial initiative. (Schein, 1988: 11)

Looking for a course that would provide what Schein describes is the point. It would be even better if the course also included some substance and practice on interpersonal and intergroup conflict.

12. *Organization theory.* This course should follow the basic course on organizational behavior or organizational psychology. Usually this kind of course helps one learn about organizational design, effectiveness (performance criteria), and the organization as a system.

13. *Functions of organizations.* This course might be subtitled "crash course in business." I have designed and conducted such a course, the latter, one for our organizational psychology graduate students at Teachers College, Columbia University. I joke about it as an MBA degree in one semester. The students do not see it as amusing. The course is designed for students who have no background in business or in how organizations actually function. Thus, there are classes on accounting, finance, budgeting, operations, marketing, strategy, and the manager's role. I also tell students that it is a course about learning a new language. The point is this: I believe strongly that to be effective as an organizational psychologist, in general, and as an organization consultant, in particular, one needs to know at least some of the basics about how organizations operate and function as well as the language of management.

I purposely limited myself to twelve or thirteen courses, conforming to a typical master's degree program requiring thirty-six to forty credits. Pepperdine University's nonresidential master of science in organization development program is an example, although that program's curriculum and what I have outlined are not exactly the same. Prerequisite to the thirteen courses I have listed is an undergraduate degree in psychology, sociology, or anthropology.

Nonacademic Training

Several professional development programs are offered by training organizations or by the continuing education divisions of universities. These provide useful training in both the knowledge and the skill appropriate to OD practice, but the weight is usually on the side of skill development. The following are ten avenues or programs for developing oneself toward becoming an OD practitioner:

1. *Basic laboratory training program.* This involves attending at least a five-day event devoted to improving one's interpersonal competence—a T-group, Gestalt group, a Tavistock group, or something very similar.

2. *Personal growth laboratory.* The first program listed emphasizes interpersonal development, whereas this one focuses on intrapersonal understanding. Since the primary instrument in OD work is the consultant practitioner, it is important that one know this instrument as well as possible.

3. *Training theory and practice.* This is the name of a program offered by the National Training Laboratories (NTL) Institute, and other organizations may offer a similar program. Attending such a program will provide an opportunity to learn about the design of training laboratories and the necessary skills for conducting them.

4. *Consultation skills.* Practice in consulting is imperative, and this type of program is ideal, since it offers a safe environment for testing untried skills.

5. *Organization development laboratory.* This program usually provides an introduction to the field and may range from a one-week version to a four-week one. Universities such as UCLA and the University of Michigan offer one-week programs; Teachers College, Columbia University, offers a two-week program entitled Principles and Practices of Organization Development; and organizations such as University Associates and the NTL Institute offer similar programs.

6. *Team-building programs.* Organizations such as the University of Michigan and Block–Petrella Associates offer training in how to consult with teams.

7. *Supervised experience.* Sometimes such an experience is provided as part of a consultation skills training program; otherwise, one needs to consult with an actual

client and arrange some form of supervision from an experienced OD consultant. Having a mentor is a related avenue for professional and personal development.

8. *Internal consultant with large organization.* An excellent way to get started in OD is to work for an organization that has an internal OD service for its managers. I emphasize *large* organization because the opportunities would be greater and more varied. One may not be able to join an internal OD group immediately, so the entry job should be at least closely associated with OD work, such as training, career development, or human resource planning. One can then make contacts, express interest, and arrange for an experience such as that suggested in option 7.

9. *Professional associations.* Belonging to and attending the meetings of certain associations devoted to OD can of course help one learn about and keep up with the field. Such organizations are the OD Network, the OD divisions of the American Society for Training and Development and the Academy of Management, and certain regional groups, such as those in New York, Philadelphia, Ohio, and the Bay Area in northern California.

10. *Advanced programs for professional development.* Programs such as Advanced Program in Organization Development and Human Resource Management, jointly sponsored by Teachers College, Columbia University and the University of Michigan, and Harvard's Managing Organization Effectiveness are designed for experienced OD practitioners and provide an opportunity for more advanced development.

Being an OD consultant means being a practitioner. We practice OD much as lawyers and physicians practice law and medicine, but there are no schools of organization development, no bar or boards to pass, and no licensing procedure. For a consideration of such matters, see Jones (1980). Certified Consultants, Inc. (formerly known as the International Association of Applied Social Scientists) and the OD Institute accredit OD consultants—but there is no systematic procedure or plan provided for how to become an OD specialist. Short of such a procedure or plan, I believe that some combination of academic training and professional development is the next best approach to becoming an OD consultant.

Part of the excitement of being involved in OD is the fact that, as a field, it is not all "put together" or "cut and dried." A new person coming into OD can still influence the shape, the form, and the eventual synthesis the field may take in the future. Since many OD people have higher-than-average needs to influence, and since many of us tend to distrust if not rebel against too much authority, perhaps the fact that the field of OD is still in an emergent phase is healthy (Burke, 1976; Friedlander, 1976). Opportunity still abounds.

Summary

In this chapter we have considered the role and personal characteristics of the OD consultant. The OD consultant may behave in a directive manner, perhaps even as an advocate, or, at the opposite extreme, may behave very nondirectively, serving perhaps as a reflector, primarily raising questions. For the most part, however, the OD consultant serves in a facilitative capacity, helping clients learn how to solve their own problems more effectively.

We also considered the role of the OD consultant from another perspective. Remaining marginal, at the boundary or interface between individuals, especially bosses and subordinates, and between groups and subsystems, is critical to effective consultation, at least from the vantage point of organization development practice. In this marginal role, the consultant functions in an organic way, attempting to intervene in a timely manner and according to what the client needs at the time. Consulting organically means that the practitioner must use himself or herself as an instrument—sensing client need by paying attention not only to what may be observed but also to his or her own feelings and intuitions. This form of consultation is not easy and is highly dependent on the skills of the consultant and subject to bias according to the consultant's personal values and attitudes. Obviously, the effective OD consultant will be sensitive to these issues, be aware of what values are espoused by the field he or she represents, and work hard to be consistent in word and deed.

11

New Dimensions of Organization Development

Thanks to Peters and Waterman (1982), Deal and Kennedy (1982), and Schein (1992, 1985) management today readily accepts the idea that an organization, like a nation or society, has a culture. (The more the organization represents a conglomerate we should more accurately say that it has cultures.)

More than ever, then, and even more so for the future, OD practitioners are involved in culture change, particularly when the need for such change is preceded by a management decision to seek new ways of doing business. In a recent study conducted with OD practitioners (Fagenson and Burke, 1990) culture change was highlighted as one of five primary activities of their work (the other four were management style enhancement, strategy development, technology integration, and employee development). Bear in mind that culture is just one dimension of an organization and is related not only to mission and strategy but to a number of other dimensions as well. The Burke–Litwin model described in Chapter 7 helps to maintain this perspective.

New Applications

While the emphasis on culture change now characterizes OD, very little "new OD" has been created during recent years. Team building no doubt still remains as one of if not the most common practice of OD consultants, which typically takes the form of "facilitating an off-site meeting." New to OD, however, is (1) its application in organizations that have not as a rule used this form of consulting, for example, health care providers (see, for example, Boss, 1989); (2) training in OD consulting skills for people outside the behavioral sciences or human resource domain, for example, information management and systems people and line managers; and (3) the use of more sophisticated analytical methods to interpret survey data.

With respect to use of OD in organizations where there has been no precedence, health care systems, in particular, are being attracted to OD because they are undergoing such significant changes. Many of these are hospitals in transition from nonprofit institutions to profit-oriented businesses. As most people know, health care in the United States is undergoing sweeping changes. Competent OD practitioners are in a position to help considerably with these organizational changes. Other organizations that have not utilized OD but are likely to be attracted to its use more in the future are those that are changing from a highly regulated business, such as airlines, or a government-owned organization to an unregulated business or publicly owned organization, British Airways being a recent example of the latter type of organization.

Regarding training in OD consulting skills, it is likely that OD practitioners will become more involved in training others in what they do. Others in this case are corporate staff specialists, such as human resource, information management and systems experts, who heretofore have legislated to operational people what they can and cannot do but now are expected to serve rather than dictate. Information management people represent a prototype of this new application of OD. Organizations have less need for their special knowledge as the sophistication of line, operational people grows about computer and data processing, thanks to desktop computers and networks that have replaced the behemoth mainframes of earlier times. Nonspecialists know more than was true a decade ago about what their information needs are and what they want in response to their needs. Their expectation, therefore, is that the information management specialist will facilitate their obtaining what they want rather than determining it. The same kind of change regarding the role of staff specialists is true for planning experts, market researchers, and training directors. There are no doubt other examples. The point is that with a combination of line, operational people ("clients") becoming more knowledgeable about the expertise staff specialists provide and staff specialists becoming more vulnerable to reductions in force, these staff specialists must modify their roles. Becoming more consultative and facilitative is a modification in the right direction. OD practitioners can indeed help.

And with respect to using more sophisticated methods to analyze questionnaire data, OD practitioners will be using, or clearly will *need* to be using, more powerful analytical tools to remain effective in the future. They will need to use computers and statistics other than merely averages and percentages in order to help clients understand more thoroughly the complexities, subtle nuances, and potential implications of organizational behavior. Gathering and analyzing data from numerous sources is particularly pertinent to large, multicultural organizations where information from one segment explains very little about the total system. For an example of such analytical methods used in an OD context, see Bernstein and Burke (1989).

And now to end this chapter and the book, we will return to values first discussed in Chapter 10. This return to values addresses perhaps *the* value dilemma for OD practitioners; even so, we conclude with a *normative* view.

The Value Dilemma for OD

I have stated that OD is a process of cultural change and that the value system of an organization is a significant component of its culture. For the organization to change significantly, then, its values must change. To what values should it change? What would the new culture look like? Who determines the direction and desired end state for the change? Is OD a body of knowledge and practice that helps managers and administrators to bring about change regardless of direction? Are OD practitioners facilitators only? Or does the field of organization development represent a certain direction of change, an implied if not clear-cut desired end state? Practitioners and academics in organization development are divided on these questions. Most believe in a contingent approach to OD, but some argue for a normative approach. The contingent camp argues that OD practitioners should only facilitate change, not focus it. They believe that the client should determine the direction of change, and the consultant should help the client to get there. Moreover, they argue, there is no one best way to organize—to structure an organization—no one best way to manage people, and no one best way to design, for example, an organization's reward system. The course of these directional decisions depends on many factors: the organization's environment, the nature of the work force, the organization's type of business or service, and so forth.

Those who argue for a normative approach, a much smaller group, believe that, although the consultative approach should be facilitative at the outset, the consultant-practitioner eventually should begin to recommend and encourage specific directions for change.

The value dilemma in OD—contingent versus normative—is manifested in different ways. Tichy (1974), for example, found that, compared with three other types of consultants or change agents, OD consultants were highest in value-action incongruence. The OD consultants believed that they should encourage if not push for humanistic and *participative management practices,* but, in practice, they admitted that they were primarily concerned with the more traditional and typical problems of how to increase efficiency and productivity. Take, for example, the problem of what is called organizational downsizing (or what some even more euphemistically call rightsizing). What stance should OD practitioners take regarding layoffs— assuming they are not among those losing their jobs? Is letting people go humanistic? At least one person related to the field, Jerry Harvey, has stated that letting people go under circumstances of downsizing is immoral (Harvey, 1988: ch. 6). Perhaps it is; in any case, people can be treated more humanely under these conditions than is usually the case. Moreover, a minimal *should* for OD practitioners as far as I am concerned is to be knowledgeable about the psychological consequences for people involved in a downsizing situation. Two of the best sources I know for gaining the relevant knowledge are Kissler (1991) and Brockner (1992). Armed with knowledge, at least OD practitioners would be in position to make authoritative interventions and more humane ones regarding the downsizing process.

In concluding their excellent review of the status of organization development, Friedlander and Brown (1974) stated that "the future of OD rests in part on its values and the degree to which its practice, theory, and research are congruent with those values" (p. 355).

It may be that the value dilemma of contingent versus normative is not a conflict, as one at first might think. I agree that the consultant should be facilitative, especially at the beginning of an OD effort. For me the cardinal principle of entry-level consultation is to take the client where he or she is. The consultant must deal first with the client's problems or hurts. As more is learned about the organization's culture, especially its norms and values, and if the consultant is knowledgeable about behavioral science theory and research, he or she gradually moves closer to being able to make authoritative interventions. The consultant does not make the directional decisions for change but suggests certain directions to the client and, then, if the client agrees, works closely with him or her to help implement the changes. As authoritative consultants we must be selective, of course, first determining the client's readiness for change (which was clearly not the situation described in the case in Chapter 1) and then deciding which areas of behavioral science knowledge are also applicable in a given situation. We must be selective for another reason also: our applicable knowledge is meager but, compared with what most other managers and administrators know about applied behavioral science, we are or should be in a more authoritative position.

A Normative View of OD

The final question to be addressed regarding the issue of contingent versus normative organization development is what normative is. What norm should we advocate when we are implementing change in an organization's culture?

The normative shift concerns values more than any other aspect of the organization's culture. Changes in certain norms would support value shifts that had already been determined. The shift is generally toward a more humanistic treatment of members at all levels in the organization. More specifically, the direction of change would be toward an organizational culture with the following characteristics:

1. Growth and development of organization members is just as important as making a profit or meeting the budget.

2. Equal opportunity and fairness for people in the organization is commonplace; it is the rule rather than the exception.

3. Managers exercise their authority more participatively than unilaterally and arbitrarily, and authority is associated more with knowledge and competence than role or status.

4. Cooperative behavior is rewarded more frequently than competitive behavior.

5. Organization members are kept informed or at least have access to information, especially concerning matters that directly affect their jobs or them personally.

6. Members feel a sense of ownership of the organization's mission and objectives.

7. Conflict is dealt with openly and systematically, rather than ignored, avoided, or handled in a typical win-lose fashion.

8. Rewards are based on a system of both equality-fairness and equity-merit.

9. Organization members are given as much autonomy and freedom to do their respective jobs as possible, to ensure both a high degree of individual motivation and accomplishment of organizational objectives.

Although this list is more value-laden, it is not unlike Beckhard's (1969) characteristics of an effective organization:

1. The total organization, the significant subparts, and individuals manage their work against *goals* and *plans* for achievement of these goals.

2. Form follows function; that is, the program or task or project determines how the human resources are organized.

3. Decisions are made by and near the sources of information, regardless of where these sources are located on the organizational chart.

4. The reward system is such that managers and supervisors are rewarded or punished comparably for short-

term profit or production performance, growth, and development of the subordinates, and creating a viable working group.

5. Lateral and vertical communication is relatively undistorted. People are generally open and confronting. They share all the relevant facts, including feelings.

6. There is a minimum of inappropriate win-lose activities between individuals and groups. Constant effort is made at all levels to treat conflict and conflict situations as *problems,* subject to problem-solving methods.

7. There is high conflict (clash of ideas) about tasks and projects and relatively little energy spent in clashing over *interpersonal* difficulties, because they generally have been worked through.

8. The organization and its parts see themselves as interacting with each other and with a larger environment. The organization is an open system.

9. There is a shared view, and management strategy to support it, of trying to help each person or unit in the organization to maintain integrity and uniqueness in an interdependent environment.

10. The organization and its members operate in an action-research way. General practice is to build in *feedback mechanisms* so that individuals and groups can learn from their own experience.

A different but compatible perspective on the nature of an effective organization—what a new culture that operationalized many of the values I've covered would look like—is provided by Peter Vaill's (1989) description of "high-performing systems." His theory base and perspective is steeped in the sociotechnical systems context, especially the notion of joint optimization.

My coverage of the nature or end state of the cultural change is still very general and perhaps even vague, but OD remains relatively young as a field and additional experience, theory, and research will provide greater specificity and clarity. It is best, therefore, to consider these characteristics of a new organizational culture as preliminary. It should be clear that normative change primarily concerns values; other aspects of change, such as organizational structure, the substance of a fringe benefit package, the design of a management information system, or a decision to install a new reward system, are all contingent matters. If puzzling questions remain about the specific directions of some of these latter examples of change, however— if "what it depends on" is unclear or does not appear to matter much—a guide should be sought from within the value system to which the organization aspires.

A most appropriate question about my coverage and viewpoint regarding organizational value and change is: What right do I have to say what an organization's values should be, to impose my values on anyone else? Fundamentally, I have no such right. For me to assume that I can act as a value-free consultant, however, is pure nonsense. It is most important for me to work toward as much clarity of my values as possible and to declare these values relatively early in the consultant-client relationship. Most are clear anyway if the client has paid any attention to my behavior and to my recommendations. I believe this fear of imposition is a false obstacle. As a perceived expert, I have a certain amount of power, but I have never had a client who was unable to say no to me.

Regarding value change, then, OD values are in line with societal shifts that are already under way. In some respects, OD practitioners are simply trying to catch up with and respond to these shifts. Recent research evidence and certain theories in the behavioral sciences are also compatible with many of these value changes.

Three Conclusions

First, OD as a field has a bright future. The primary reason being that societal and corporate trends are converging more within OD values and with what OD practitioners have to offer. Revisiting Chapter 2 and considering what Naisbett, Peters, Kanter, and I view as the changes that are already under way, we can easily see that OD is not only compatible but positioned to be in the mainstream. Moreover, the quality movement, to be successful, is highly dependent on effective process—and process is the OD practitioner's most important product. These are but a few examples. The point is that OD, or whatever it may be labeled in the distant future, is here to stay.

Second, we clearly have a set of standard tools that effectively address small- to medium-size problems in organizations today. A client says, "I am really having a tough time with my subordinates. I think I'll call our OD consultant for some team-building help." Another may say, "We are having difficulty with our customer service. We may be organized inappropriately. I think I'll check in with our OD group for some help." We have standard ways of facilitating teamwork and for looking at people's work responsibilities to see how they fit or do not fit together with other people's work responsibilities. Moreover, we can train people in these consulting skills. We know how to do it (Burke, 1991).

The third conclusion is quite different. OD practitioners are beginning to face in another direction, not a direction that is incompatible with where we are today, noted above, but different. We are on the threshold of a paradigm for the effective management of large-scale organization change. Large-scale system change has been written about before (for example, Beckhard and Harris, 1987), but now we are beginning to understand much more clearly what the primary levers are for initiating and implementing organization change, levers such as culture, values, key leadership acts (providing a vision and clear sense of direction), the reward system, and management/executive programs. Think about what I am trying to say this way: Traveling in a car you have no doubt experienced fog on the road. The experience can produce considerable anxiety. My most memorable experience in fog occurred while navigating my boat: Not being sure of just where I was regardless of compass reading or what was about to emerge as I proceeded ever so cautiously through the water was more than a bit frightening. Anxiety changes to elation when the fog begins to lift and one can see the surroundings and the way to proceed.

These are exciting times in OD because greater clarity about the complexities and paradoxes regarding organization change and how to deal with them is gradually beginning to emerge. The fog is lifting.

References

Ackoff, R. L. 1981. *Creating the Corporate Future*. New York: Wiley.

Adizes, I. 1979. "Organizational Passages: Diagnosing and Treating Lifecycle Problems of Organizations." *Organizational Dynamics* 8(1): 2–25.

Allport, G. W. 1945. *The Nature of Prejudice*. Cambridge, Mass.: Addison-Wesley.

Argyris, C. 1971. *Management and Organizational Development*. New York: McGraw-Hill.

———. 1970. *Intervention Theory and Method*. Reading, Mass.: Addison-Wesley.

———. 1968. "Some Unintended Consequences of Rigorous Research." *Psychological Bulletin* 7: 185–97.

———. 1962. *Interpersonal Competence and Organizational Effectiveness*. Homewood, Ill.: Dorsey Press.

Argyris, C., R. Putnam, and D. M. Smith. 1985. *Action Science*. San Francisco: Jossey-Bass.

Argyris, C., and D. A. Schön. 1978. *Organizational Learning: A Theory of Action Perspective*. Reading, Mass.: Addison-Wesley.

"At Emery Air Freight: Positive Reinforcement Boosts Performance." 1973. *Organizational Dynamics* 1(3): 41–67.

Bass, B. M. 1985. *Leadership and Performance Beyond Expectations*. New York: The Free Press.

Beckhard, R. 1969. *Organization Development: Strategies and Models*. Reading, Mass.: Addison-Wesley.

———. 1967. "The Confrontation Meeting." *Harvard Business Review* 45(2): 149–55.

Beckhard, R., and R. T. Harris. 1987. *Organizational Transitions: Managing Complex Change.* 2nd ed. Reading, Mass.: Addison-Wesley.

———. 1977. *Organizational Transitions: Managing Complex Change.* Reading, Mass.: Addison-Wesley.

Beckhard, R., and D. G. Lake. 1971. "Short- and Long-Range Effects of a Team Development Effort." In H. A. Hornstein, B. B. Bunker, W. W. Burke, M. Gindes, and R. J. Lewicki, eds., *Social Interventions: A Behavioral Science Approach.* New York: Free Press, pp. 421–39.

Beckhard, R., and W. Pritchard. 1992. *Changing the Essence: The Art of Creating and Leading Fundamental Change in Organizations.* San Francisco: Jossey-Bass.

Bennis, W. G., and B. Nanus. 1985. *Leaders: The Strategies for Taking Charge.* New York: Harper & Row.

Bernstein, W. M., and W. W. Burke. 1989. "Modeling Organizational Meaning Systems." In R. W. Woodman and W. A. Pasmore, eds., *Research in Organizational Change and Development.* Greenwich, Conn.: JAI Press, pp. 117–59.

Bion, W. R. 1961. *Experiences in Groups.* New York: Basic Books.

Blake, R. R., and J. S. Mouton. 1982. "A Comparative Analysis of Situationalism and 9,9 Management by Principle." *Organizational Dynamics* 10(4): 20–43.

———. 1981. *Toward Resolution of the Situationalism vs. "One Best Style . . ." Controversy in Leadership Theory, Research, and Practice.* Austin: Scientific Methods.

———. 1978. *The New Managerial Grid.* Houston: Gulf.

———. 1968. *Corporate Excellence Through Grid Organization Development.* Houston: Gulf.

———. 1964. *The Managerial Grid.* Houston: Gulf.

Blake, R. R., J. S. Mouton, L. B. Barnes, and L. E. Greiner. 1964. "Breakthrough in Organizational Development." *Harvard Business Review* 42: 133–55.

Boss, R. W. 1989. *Organization Development in Health Care.* Reading, Mass.: Addison-Wesley.

Bowers, D. G. 1973. "OD Techniques and Their Results in 23 Organizations: The Michigan ICL Study." *Journal of Applied Behavioral Science* 9:21–43.

Brockner, J. 1988. *Self-Esteem at Work: Research, Theory and Practice.* Lexington, Mass.: Lexington Books.

Brockner, J. 1992 "Managing the Effects of Layoffs on Survivors." *California Management Review* 34(2): 9–28.

Brockner, J., L. Greenberg, A. Brockner, J. Bortz, J. Davy, and C. Carter. 1986. "Layoffs, Equity Theory and Work Performance: Further Evidence of the Impact of Survivor Guilt." *Academy of Management Journal* 29: 373–84.

Brown, L. D. 1972. "Research Action: Organizational Feedback, Understanding, and Change." *Journal of Applied Behavioral Science* 8: 697–711.

Burck, G. 1965. "Union Carbide's Patient Schemers." *Fortune* (December): 147–49.

Burke, W. W. 1993. "The Changing World of Organization Change." *Consulting Psychology Journal* 45(1): 9–17.

——. 1991. "Practicing Organization Development." In *Working with Organizations and Their People: A Guide to Human Resources Practice.* D. W. Bray and Associates, New York: Guilford, pp. 95–130.

——. 1986. "Leadership as Empowering Others." In *Executive Power: How Executives Influence People and Organizations.* S. Srivastva and Associates. San Francisco: Jossey-Bass, pp. 51–77.

——. 1982. *Organization Development: Principles and Practices.* Boston: Little, Brown.

——. 1980. "Systems Theory, Gestalt Therapy, and Organization Development." In T. G. Cummings, ed. *Systems Training for Organization Development.* London: John Wiley and Sons, pp. 209–22.

——. 1976. "Organization Development in Transition." *Journal of Applied Behavioral Science* 12: 22–43.

——. 1974. "Managing Conflict Between Groups." In J. D. Adams, ed., *New Technologies in Organizational Development: 2.* San Diego: University Associates, pp. 255–68.

Burke, W. W., L. P. Clark, and C. Koopman. 1984. "Improve Your OD Project's Chances for Success." *Training and Development Journal* 38(8): 62–68.

Burke, W. W., and H. A. Hornstein, eds. 1972. *The Social Technology of Organization Development.* La Jolla, Calif.: University Associates.

Burke, W. W., and P. Jackson. 1991. "Making the Smith Kline Beecham Merger Work." *Human Resource Management* 30: 69–87.

Burke, W. W., and G. H. Litwin. 1992. "A Causal Model of Organizational Performance and Change." *Journal of Management* 18(3): 532–45.

——. 1989. "A Causal Model of Organizational Change and Performance." In J. W. Pfeiffer, ed., *1989 Annual: Developing Human Resources.* San Diego: University Associates, pp. 277–88.

Burke, W. W., and R. A. Myers. 1982. *Assessment of Executive Competence.* Technical Report. Washington, D.C.: National Aeronautics and Space Administration.

Burke, W. W., and W. H. Schmidt. 1971. "Primary Target for Change: The Manager or the Organization?" In H. A. Hornstein, B. B. Bunker, W. W. Burke, M. Gindes, and R. J. Lewicki, eds., *Social Intervention: A Behavioral Science Approach.* New York: The Free Press, pp. 373–85.

Burns, J. M. 1978. *Leadership.* New York: Harper & Row.

Burns, J. M., and G. Stalker. 1961. *The Management of Innovation.* London: Tavistock.

Bushe, G. R., and A. B. Shani. 1991. *Parallel Learning Structures: Increasing Innovation in Bureaucracies.* Reading, Mass.: Addison-Wesley.

Cameron, K. 1980. "Critical Questions in Assessing Organizational Effectiveness." *Organizational Dynamics* 9(2): 66–80.

Campbell, T. D., and J. C. Stanley. 1966. *Experimental and Quasi-Experimental Designs for Research.* Chicago: Rand McNally.

Capra, F. 1983. *The Turning Point: Science, Society, and the Rising Culture.* New York: Bantam Books.

——. 1977. "The Tao of Physics: Reflections on the 'Cosmic Dance'." *Saturday Review* 5(6): 21–23, 28.

——. 1976. *The Tao of Physics: An Exploration of the Parallels Between Modern Physics and Eastern Mysticism.* 2nd ed. Boulder, Colo.: Shambhala Publications.

Carlzon, J. 1987. *Moments of Truth: New Strategies for Today's Customer-Driven Economy.* Cambridge, Mass.: Ballinger.

Chandler, A. 1962. *Strategy and Structure.* Cambridge, Mass.: MIT Press.

Church, A. H., and W. W. Burke. 1993. "What Are the Basic Values of OD?" *Academy of Management ODC Division Newsletter.* Winter: 1, 7–11.

Church, A. H., W. W. Burke, and D. F. Van Eynde. 1994. "Values, Motives, and Interventions of Organization Development Practitioners." *Group and Organization Management.* In Press.

Coch, L., and J. R. P. French. 1948. "Overcoming Resistance to Change." *Human Relations* 1: 512–32.

Collier, J. 1945. "United States Indian Administration as a Laboratory of Ethnic Relations." *Social Research* 12 (May): 275–76.

Davis, S. A. 1967. "An Organic Problem-Solving Method of Organizational Change." *Journal of Applied Behavioral Science* 3: 3–21.

Deal, T. E., and A. A. Kennedy. 1982. *Corporate Cultures: The Rites and Rituals of Corporate Life.* Reading, Mass.: Addison-Wesley.

Dowling, W. F. 1975. "System 4 Builds Performance and Profits." *Organizational Dynamics* 3(3): 23–38.

Duvall, S., and R. A. Wicklund. 1972. *A Theory of Objective Self Awareness.* New York: Academic Press.

Fagenson, E. A., and W. W. Burke. 1990. "Organization Development Practitioners' Activities and Interventions in Organizations During the 1980s." *Journal of Applied Behavioral Science* 26: 285–97.

Foltz, J. A., J. B. Harvey, and J. McLaughlin. 1974. "Organization Development: A Line Management Function." In J. D. Adams, ed., *Theory and Method in Organization Development: An Evolutionary Process.* Arlington, Va.: NTL Institute, pp. 373–85.

Fox, M. M. 1990. The Role of Individual Perceptions of Organizational Culture in Predicting Perceptions of Work Unit Climate and Organizational Performance. Unpublished doctoral dissertation, Columbia University, New York.

French, W. L. 1969. "Organization Development: Objectives, Assumptions, and Strategies." *California Management Review* 12: 23–34.

French, W. L., and C. H. Bell, Jr. 1978. *Organization Development,* 2nd ed. Englewood Cliffs, N.J.: Prentice-Hall.

Friedlander, F. 1976. "OD Reaches Adolescence: An Exploration of Its Underlying Values." *Journal of Applied Behavioral Science* 12(1): 7–21.

———. 1970. "The Primacy of Trust as a Facilitator of Further Group Accomplishment." *Journal of Applied Behavioral Science* 6: 387–400.

Friedlander, F., and L. D. Brown. 1974. "Organization Development." *Annual Review of Psychology* 25: 313–41.

Frohman, M. A., M. Sashkin, and M. J. Kavanagh. 1976. "Action Research as Applied to Organization Development." *Organization and Administrative Sciences* 7: 129–42.

Frost, P. J., L. F. Moore, M. R. Louis, C. C. Lundberg, and J. Martin, eds. 1991. *Reframing Organizational Culture*. Newbury Park, Calif.: Sage Publications.

Gabarro, J. J., and J. P. Kotter. 1980. "Managing Your Boss." *Harvard Business Review* (January-February): 92–100.

Galbraith, J. R. 1982. "Designing the Innovating Organization." *Organizational Dynamics* 10(1): 5–25.

——. *Organization Design*. Reading, Mass.: Addison-Wesley.

Greiner, L. E. 1972. "Evolution and Revolution as Organizations Grow." *Harvard Business Review* 50(4): 37–46.

Gleick, J. 1987. *Chaos: Making a New Science*. New York: Viking.

Golembiewski, R. T., K. Billingsley, and S. Yeager. 1976. "Measuring Change and Persistence in Human Affairs: Types of Change Generated by OD Designs." *Journal of Applied Behavioral Science* 12: 133–57.

Golembiewski, R. T., R. Hilles, and M. S. Kagno. 1974. "A Longitudinal Study of Flex-time Effects: Some Consequences of an OD Structural Intervention." *Journal of Applied Behavioral Science* 10: 503–32.

Goodman, P. S., and J. M. Pennings. 1980. "Critical Issues in Assessing Organizational Effectiveness." In E. E. Lawler, D. A. Nadler, and C. Cammann, eds., *Organizational Assessment: Perspectives on the Measurement of Organizational Behavior and the Quality of Work Life*. New York: Wiley-Interscience, pp. 185–215.

Goodstein, L. D., and W. W. Burke. 1991. "Creating Successful Organizational Change." *Organizational Dynamics* 19(4): 5–17.

Greiner, L. E. 1972. "Evolution and Revolution as Organizations Grow." *Harvard Business Review* 50(4): 37–46.

Guzzo, R. A., R. D. Jette, and R. A. Katzell. 1985. "The Effects of Psychologically Based Intervention Programs on Worker Productivity: A Meta-analysis." *Personnel Psychology* 38: 275–91.

Hackman, J. R., ed. 1989. *Groups That Work (and Those That Don't): Creating Conditions for Effective Teamwork*. San Francisco: Jossey-Bass.

Hackman, J. R., and G. R. Oldham. 1980. *Work Redesign*. Reading, Mass.: Addison-Wesley.

——. 1975. "Development of the Job Diagnostic Survey." *Journal of Applied Psychology* 60: 159–70.

Hall, J. 1976. "To Achieve or Not: The Manager's Choice." *California Management Review* 18(4): 5–18.

Hanna, D. P. 1988. *Designing Organizations for High Performance.* Reading, Mass.: Addison-Wesley.

Harvey, J. B. 1988. *The Abilene Paradox and Other Meditations on Management.* Lexington, Mass.: Lexington Books.

——. 1974. "The Abilene Paradox: The Management of Agreement." *Organizational Dynamics* 3(2): 63–80.

Heisler, W. J. 1975. "Patterns of OD in Practice." *Business Horizons* (February): 77–84.

Herzberg, F. 1966. *Work and the Nature of Man.* Cleveland: World.

Herzberg, F., B. Mausner, and B. Snyderman. 1959. *The Motivation to Work.* New York: Wiley.

Homans, G. C. 1950. *The Human Group.* New York: Harcourt, Brace.

Hornstein, H. A., B. B. Bunker, W. W. Burke, M. Gindes, and R. J. Lewicki. 1971. *Social Intervention: A Behavioral Science Approach.* New York: Free Press.

Hornstein, H. A., and N. M. Tichy. 1973. *Organization Diagnosis and Improvement Strategies.* New York: Behavioral Science Associates.

Jamieson, D., and J. O'Mara. 1991. *Managing Workforce 2000: Gaining the Diversity Advantage.* San Francisco: Jossey-Bass.

Jantsch, E. 1980. *The Self-Organizing Universe: Scientific and Human Implications of the Emerging Paradigm of Evolution.* Elmsford, N.Y.: Pergamon Press.

Jones, J. E. 1980. "Quality Control of OD Practitioners and Practice." In W. W. Burke and L. D. Goodstein, eds., *Trends and Issues in OD: Current Theory and Practice.* San Diego: University Associates, pp. 333–45.

Kanter, R. M. 1989. *When Giants Learn to Dance: Mastering the Challenges of Strategy, Management, and Careers in the 1990s.* New York: Simon and Schuster.

——. 1984. *The Change Masters: Innovating for Productivity in the American Corporation.* New York: Warner Books.

——. 1982. "Dilemmas of Managing Participation." *Organizational Dynamics* 11(1): 5–27.

Katz, D., and R. L. Kahn. 1978. *The Social Psychology of Organizations.* 2nd ed. New York: Wiley.

Kimberly, J. R., and W. R. Nielsen. 1975. "Organization Development and Change in Organizational Performance." *Administrative Science Quarterly* 20: 191–206.

King, A. 1974. "Expectation Effects in Organizational Change." *Administrative Science Quarterly* 19: 221–30.

King, D.C., J. J. Sherwood, and M. R. Manning. 1978. "OD's Research Base: How to Expand and Utilize It." In W. W. Burke, ed., *The Cutting Edge: Current Theory and Practice in Organization Development.* La Jolla, Calif.: University Associates, pp. 133–48.

Kissler, G. D. 1991. *The Change Riders: Managing the Power of Change.* Reading, Mass.: Addison-Wesley.

Kolb, D., and A. Frohman. 1970. "An Organization Development Approach to Consulting." *Sloan Management Review* 12(1): 51–65.

Kotter, J. P. 1982. *The General Managers.* New York: The Free Press.

Kotter, J. P., and J. L. Heskett. 1992. *Corporate Culture and Performance.* New York: The Free Press.

Lawler, E. E. III. 1992. *The Ultimate Advantage: Creating the High Involvement Organization.* San Francisco: Jossey-Bass.

———. 1977. "Reward Systems." In J. R. Hackman and J. L. Suttle, eds., *Improving Life at Work.* Santa Monica, Calif.: Goodyear, pp. 163–226.

———. 1973. *Motivation in Work Organizations.* Monterey, Calif.: Brooks/Cole.

Lawrence, P. R., and J. W. Lorsch. 1969. *Developing Organizations: Diagnosis and Action.* Reading, Mass.: Addison-Wesley.

———. 1967. *Organization and Environment: Managing Differentiation and Integration.* Boston: Division of Research, Harvard Business School.

Leahey, J., and J. P. Kotter. 1990. *Changing the Culture at British Airways.* Harvard Business School Case No. 491–009.

Levinson, H. 1975. *Executive Stress.* New York: Harper & Row.

———. 1972a. *Organizational Diagnosis.* Cambridge, Mass.: Harvard University Press.

———. 1972b. "The Clinical Psychologist as Organizational Diagnostician." *Professional Psychology* 3: 34–40.

Lewicki, R. J., and C. P. Alderfer. 1973. "The Tensions Between Research and Intervention in Intergroup Conflict." *Journal of Applied Behavioral Science* 9(4): 423–68.

Lewin, K. 1958. "Group Decision and Social Change." In E. E. Maccoby, T. M. Newcomb, and E. L. Hartley, eds., *Readings in Social Psychology*. New York: Holt, Rinehart, and Winston, pp. 163–226.

———. 1951. *Field Theory in Social Science*. New York: Harper.

———. 1948. *Resolving Social Conflicts*. New York: Harper.

———. 1946. "Action Research and Minority Problems." *Journal of Social Issues* 2: 34–46.

———. 1936. *Principles of Topological Psychology*. New York: McGraw-Hill.

Likert, R. 1967. *The Human Organization*. New York: McGraw-Hill.

———. 1961. *New Patterns of Management*. New York: McGraw-Hill.

Lippitt, R., and G. Lippitt. 1975. "Consulting Process in Action." *Training and Development Journal* 29(5): 48–54; 29(6): 38–44.

Lippitt, R., J. Watson, and B. Westley. 1958. *Dynamics of Planned Change*. New York: Harcourt, Brace.

Litwin, G. H., and R. A. Stringer. 1969. *Motivation and Organizational Climate*. Boston: Harvard Business School Press.

Lodahl, T. M., and L. K. Williams. 1978. "An Opportunity for OD: The Office Revolution." *OD Practitioner* 10(4): 9–11.

Maccoby, M. 1976. *The Gamesman: The New Corporate Leaders*. New York: Irvington.

McClelland, D. C. 1975. *Power: The Inner Experience*. New York: Irvington.

McGregor, D. 1967. *The Professional Manager*. New York: McGraw-Hill.

———. 1960. *The Human Side of Enterprise*. New York: McGraw-Hill.

Mann, F. C. 1957. "Studying and Creating Change: A Means to Understanding Social Organization." In *Research in Industrial Human Relations*. Industrial Relations Research Association, Publication No. 17.

Margulies, N. 1978. "Perspectives on the Marginality of the Consultant's Role." In W. W. Burke, ed., *The Cutting Edge: Current Theory and Practice in Organization Development*. La Jolla, Calif.: University Associates, pp. 60–69.

Marrow, A. J. 1969. *The Practical Theorist*. New York: Basic Books.

Marrow, A. J., D. G. Bowers, and S. E. Seashore. 1967. *Management by Participation*. New York: Harper & Row.

Maslow, A. H. 1965. *Eupsychian Management: A Journal.* Homewood, Ill.: Richard I. Irwin, and the Dorsey Press.

———. 1954. *Motivation and Personality.* New York: Harper & Brothers.

Mayo, E. 1933. *The Human Problems of an Industrial Civilization.* Boston: Harvard University Graduate School of Business.

Michela, J. L., S. M. Boni, C. B. Schechter, G. Manderlink, W. M. Bernstein, M. O'Malley, and W. W. Burke. 1988. A Hierarchically Nested Model for Estimation of Influences on Organizational Climate: Rationale, Methods, and Demonstration. Working Paper, Teachers College, Columbia University.

Miller, E. C. 1978. "The Parallel Organization Structure at General Motors: An Interview with Howard C. Carlson." *Personnel* 55(4): 64–69.

Morrison, P. 1978. "Evaluation in OD: A Review and an Assessment." *Group and Organization Studies* 3: 42–70.

Nadler, D. A. 1981. "Managing Organizational Change: An Integrative Approach." *Journal of Applied Behavioral Science* 17(2): 191–211.

———. 1977. *Feedback and Organization Development: Using Data-Based Methods.* Reading, Mass.: Addison-Wesley.

Nadler, D. A., M. S. Gerstein, R. B. Shaw, and Associates. 1992. *Organizational Architecture: Designs for Changing Organizations.* San Francisco: Jossey-Bass.

Nadler, D. A., and M. L. Tushman. 1989. "Organizational Frame Bending: Principles for Managing Reorientation." *Academy of Management Executive* 3: 194–204.

———. 1977. "A Diagnostic Model for Organization Behavior." In J. R. Hackman, E. E. Lawler, and L. W. Porter, eds., *Perspectives on Behavior in Organizations.* New York: McGraw-Hill, pp. 85–100.

Naisbett, J. 1982. *Megatrends: Ten New Directions Transforming Our Lives.* New York: Warner Books.

Naisbett, J., and P. Aburdene. 1985. *Re-inventing the Corporation.* New York: Warner Books.

Neuman, G. A., J. E. Edwards, and N. S. Raju. 1989. "Organizational Development Interventions: A Meta-analysis of Their Effects on Satisfaction and Other Attitudes." *Personnel Psychology* 42: 461–89.

Nicolis, G., and I. Prigogine. 1977. *Self-Organization in Nonequilibrium Systems: From Dissipative Structures to Order Through Fluctations.* New York: Wiley-Interscience.

Pate, L. E., W. R. Nielsen, and P. C. Bacon. 1977. "Advances in Research on Organization Development: Toward a Beginning." *Group and Organization Studies* 2: 449–60.

Peters, T. J. 1987. *Thriving on Chaos: Handbook for a Management Revolution.* New York: Alfred A. Knopf.

Peters, T. J., and R. H. Waterman, Jr. 1982. *In Search of Excellence: Lessons from America's Best-Run Companies.* New York: Harper & Row.

Pfeiffer, J. W., and J. E. Jones. 1978. "OD Readiness." In W. W. Burke, ed., *The Cutting Edge: Current Theory and Practice in Organization Development.* La Jolla, Calif.: University Associates, pp. 179–85.

Porras, J. I. 1979. "The Comparative Impact of Different OD Techniques and Intervention Intensities." *Journal of Applied Behavioral Science* 15: 156–78.

Porras, J. I., and K. Patterson. 1979. "Assessing Planned Change." *Group and Organization Studies* 4: 39–58.

Porras, J. I., and A. Wilkens. 1980. "Organization Development in a Large System: An Empirical Assessment." *Journal of Applied Behavoral Science* 16: 506–34.

Pucik, V., N. M. Tichy, and C. K. Barnett, eds. 1992. *Globalizing Management: Creating and Leading the Competitive Organization.* New York: Wiley.

Rhinesmith, S. H. 1992. *A Manager's Guide to Globalization.* Homewood, Ill.: Business One Irwin.

Rice, A. K. 1958. *Productivity and Social Organizations: The Ahmedabad Experiment.* London: Tavistock.

Rioch, M. J. 1970. "The Work of Wilfred Bion on Groups." *Psychiatry* 33: 56–66.

Roethlisberger, F. J., and W. J. Dickson. 1939. *Management and the Worker: An Account of a Research Program Conducted by the Western Electric Company.* Cambridge, Mass.: Harvard University Press.

Rosenthal, R. 1976. *Experimenter Effects in Behavioral Research,* enlarged ed. New York: Halsted Press.

Rubin, I. 1967. "Increasing Self-Acceptance: A Means of Reducing Prejudice." *Journal of Personality and Social Psychology* 5: 233–38.

Saparito, B. 1986. "The Revolt Against 'Working Smarter'." *Fortune* 114(2): 58–65.

Sashkin, M. 1984. "Participative Management Is an Ethical Imperative." *Organizational Dynamics* 12(4): 4–22.

Sashkin, M., and W. W. Burke. 1987. "Organization Development in the 1980s." *Journal of Management* 13: 393–417.

Sashkin, M., and K. J. Kiser. 1993. *Putting Total Quality Management to Work*. San Francisco: Berrett-Kohler Publishers.

Schacter, S. 1959. *The Psychology of Affiliation*. Stanford, Calif.: Stanford University Press.

Schein, E. H. 1992. *Organizational Culture and Leadership*. 2nd ed. San Francisco: Jossey-Bass.

——. 1991. "Legitimizing Clinical Research in the Study of Organizational Culture." Sixteenth Annual Frederick J. Gaudet Lecture, Stevens Institute, Hoboken, N.J. (April 30, 1991).

——. 1988. *Process Consultation, Vol. 1: Its Role in Organization Development*. 2nd ed. Reading, Mass.: Addison-Wesley.

——. 1987. *Process Consultation, Vol. 2: Lessons for Managers and Consultants*. Reading, Mass.: Addison-Wesley.

——. 1985. *Organizational Culture and Leadership*. San Francisco: Jossey-Bass.

——. 1980. *Organizational Psychology*. 3rd ed. Englewood Cliffs, N.J.: Prentice-Hall.

——. 1969. *Process Consultation*. Reading, Mass.: Addison-Wesley.

Schein, E. H., and W. G. Bennis. 1965. *Personal and Organizational Change Through Group Methods: The Laboratory Approach*. New York: Wiley.

Schneider, B. 1990. "The Climate for Service: Application of the Construct." In B. Schneider, ed., *Organizational Climate and Culture*. San Francisco: Jossey-Bass, pp. 383–412.

——. 1980. "The Service Organization: Climate Is Crucial. *Organizational Dynamics* 9(2): 52–65.

Schneider, B., and D. E. Bowen. 1985. "Employee and Customer Perceptions of Service in Banks: Replication and Extension." *Journal of Applied Psychology* 70: 423–33.

Schuler, R. S., and D. L. Harris. 1992. *Managing Quality: The Primer for Middle Managers*. Reading, Mass.: Addison-Wesley.

Seashore, S. E., and D. G. Bowers. 1970. "Durability of Organizational Change." *American Psychologist* 25 (March): 227–33.

Selznick, P. 1957. *Leadership in Administration*. New York: Harper & Row.

Senge, P. M. 1990. *The Fifth Discipline: The Art and Practice of the Learning Organization.* New York: Doubleday.

Shepard, H. A. 1960. "Three Management Programs and the Theory Behind Them." In *An Action Research Program for Organization Improvement.* Ann Arbor: Foundation for Research on Human Behavior.

Skinner, B. F. 1971. *Beyond Freedom and Dignity.* New York: Knopf.

———. 1953. *Science and Human Behavior.* New York: Macmillan.

———. 1948. *Walden Two.* New York: Macmillan.

Tagiuri, R., and G. H. Litwin, eds. 1968. *Organizational Climate: Explorations of a Concept.* Cambridge, Mass.: Harvard University Press.

Tannenbaum, R., and S. A. Davis. 1969. "Values, Man, and Organizations." *Industrial Management Review* 10(2): 67–83.

Taylor, J., and D. G. Bowers. 1972. *The Survey of Organizations: A Machine Scored Standardized Questionnaire Instrument.* Ann Arbor: Institute for Social Research.

Tichy, N. M. 1983. *Managing Strategic Change: Technical, Political, and Cultural Dynamics.* New York: Wiley.

———. 1978. "Demise, Absorption, or Renewal for the Future of Organization Development." In W. W. Burke, ed., *The Cutting Edge: Current Theory and Practice in Organization Development.* La Jolla, Calif.: University Associates, pp. 70–88.

———. 1974. "Agents of Planned Social Change: Congruence of Values, Cognitions, and Actions." *Administrative Science Quarterly* 19: 164–82.

Tichy, N. M., and M. A. Devanna. 1986. *The Transformational Leader.* New York: Wiley.

Tichy, N. M., H. A. Hornstein, and J. N. Nisberg. 1977. "Organization Diagnosis and Intervention Strategies: Developing Emergent Pragmatic Theories of Change." In W. W. Burke, ed., *Current Issues and Strategies in Organization Development.* New York: Human Sciences Press, pp. 361–83.

Trist, E. 1960. *Socio-technical Systems.* London: Tavistock Institute of Human Relations.

Trist, E., and K. Bamforth. 1951. "Some Social and Psychological Consequences of the Long Wall Method of Coal-Getting." *Human Relations* 4(1): 1–8.

Tushman, M. L., and D. A. Nadler. 1978. "Information Processing as an Integrative Concept in Organizational Design." *Academy of Management Review* 3: 613–24.

Vaill, P. B. 1989. *Managing as a Performing Art.* San Francisco: Jossey-Bass.

Van Eron, A. M., and W. W. Burke. 1992. "Key Components of the Transformational/Transactional Leadership Model: The Relationship Between Individual Differences, Leadership Disposition, Behavior, and Climate." In K. E. Clark and M. B. Clark, eds., *Impact of Leadership.* West Orange, N.J.: Leadership Library of America, Inc.

Vroom, V. 1964. *Work and Motivation.* New York: Wiley.

Watson, G. 1966. "Resistance to Change." In G. Watson, ed., *Concepts for Social Change,* Cooperative Project for Educational Development Series, Vol. 1. Washington, D.C.: National Training Laboratories.

Weisbord, M. R. 1978. *Organizational Diagnosis: A Workbook of Theory and Practice.* Reading, Mass.: Addison-Wesley.

——. 1977. "How Do You Know It Works If You Don't Know What It Is?" *OD Practitioner* 9(3), 1–8.

——. 1976. "Organizational Diagnosis: Six Places to Look for Trouble With or Without a Theory." *Group and Organization Studies* 1: 430–47.

——. 1973. "The Organization Development Contract." *OD Practitioner* 5(2): 1–4.

Wheatley, M. J. 1992. *Leadership and the New Science.* San Francisco: Berrett-Kohler Publishers.

Zaleznik, A. 1977. "Managers and Leaders: Are They Different?" *Harvard Business Review* 55(3): 67–78.

Zand, D. W. 1974. "Collateral Organization: A New Change Strategy." *Journal of Applied Behavioral Science* 10: 63–89.